The Riverside Literature Series

SELECTED
IDYLLS OF THE KING

THE COMING OF ARTHUR
GARETH AND LYNETTE
LANCELOT AND ELAINE
THE HOLY GRAIL
THE PASSING OF ARTHUR

EDITED, WITH INTRODUCTION AND NOTES

BY

FRANKLIN T. BAKER, A.M.

PROFESSOR OF ENGLISH IN TEACHERS COLLEGE
COLUMBIA UNIVERSITY

BOSTON   NEW YORK   CHICAGO   SAN FRANCISCO
HOUGHTON MIFFLIN COMPANY
The Riverside Press Cambridge

NEW ENLARGED EDITION

PUBLISHED 1923

The Riverside Press

CAMBRIDGE · MASSACHUSETTS

PRINTED IN THE U.S.A.

PREFACE

THE editor of this volume desires expressly not to apologize for supplying either introduction, notes, or guides to the study of the four poems which it contains. The execution of his plan may be faulty; but he is quite firm in his conviction that poems of this sort need introduction, explanatory notes, and stimulating questions for the proper study of them. The word *study* is used advisedly. A lazy, cursory reading of such poetry may edify a mind of superior type; but the average mind cannot travel here in such princely fashion. The reader may soar, if he has wings; or he may climb, if he can and will.

Not all good poetry needs such help or requires such effort; much of it speaks its immortal message simply. But Tennyson's *Idylls* are too academic, too self-conscious, often too involved or too subtle, to be understood without effort.

Such apparatus for study as is here given must not be misused. It must not be treated as more important than the poems, or taken *in toto*, or accepted as infallible. The editor's intention has been only to make convenient the ordinary information, such as books of reference give; and to suggest lines or kinds of study (or question) which may help the pupil to a livelier appreciation of the meanings and the beauties of the poetry. The teacher will probably be safe if he remembers that the real master in command in the classroom is to be not himself, or the editor, but the poet who wrote *The Idylls of the King*.

CONTENTS

ILLUSTRATIONS

INTRODUCTION

THE LIFE OF TENNYSON

WE usually like to know something of the lives of great men. Just as we like to see the men whose ability and industry have made them famous, so we like to know something of their history: their childhood, their interests, their personal appearance and qualities, and how they reached their goal. Even when the great man is only a writer, and has lived a life without exciting adventures, it is interesting to learn what he was like and how he impressed those among whom he lived. So it has become a custom in reading great books to read also the lives of their authors.

Alfred Tennyson was one of the men who helped to make the nineteenth century the wonderful century it was — wonderful in science, statesmanship, and literature. By a curious coincidence he was born in the same year, 1809, as were Poe the poet, Darwin the scientist, and Gladstone and Lincoln the statesmen. He was one of the twelve children of the Reverend Dr. George Tennyson, vicar of the church at Somersby, Lincolnshire, near the eastern coast of England.

The Tennysons were a remarkable family. The father was a scholarly man of great physical and mental vigor. The mother was clear-sighted, tender, and just. The children were alert and imaginative. In their early childhood several of them, especially Alfred, his two brothers Charles and Frederick, and two of the sisters, found pleasure not only in the customary pastimes of young people, but also in making

verses and stories for the entertainment of the rest of
the family. Later, when Alfred began to be famous,
an older writer, Leigh Hunt, hearing that three or four
others of the Tennyson family could write good verses,
said : " Here is a nest of nightingales for you ! "

Tennyson, like most men of genius, was a preco-
cious child. He began to make verses when he was
five or six years old ; before he was fourteen, he had
written many things in verse, among them an epic of
six thousand lines. Some fragments of these childish
writings that have been preserved show that he had
even then both imagination and a feeling for the
music of verse. He read much and eagerly, both in
poetry and prose. By the time he was fourteen he was
familiar with a good deal of English poetry. Byron,
then at the height of his fame, especially appealed
to him. In 1827 he and his brother Charles published
a small volume called *Poems by Two Brothers*.
Though it contained no great poetry, the verses gave
promise of the fine work that came later. It is pleasant to know that the two young authors were still
real boys ; for they at once spent a part of the money
they got for the volume in a holiday trip to the sea-
shore.

The region in which these children were brought up
was " a land of quiet villages, large fields, gray hill-
sides, and noble tall-towered churches " ; a land of
rich and quiet beauty, as are so many of the English
landscapes. Here the young poet grew into that love
of nature and that sensitiveness to beauty of which his
poetry is so full.

His early education was obtained first at a school
in Louth — a school of the vigorous type that has been
described so often in English fiction. But in a short

while he was withdrawn and taught at home. Under his father's scholarly guidance, he read in preparation for the university his Greek, Latin, and mathematics.

In 1828 Tennyson entered Trinity College at the University of Cambridge. Although a great reader then, as he was all his life, and a good student in the classics, the only honors he won were for the prize poem *Timbuctoo*, still included among his works. But the life at the University meant much more in his development than mere knowledge of books. He was one of a circle of young men who called themselves "The Apostles," and who eagerly studied and discussed many important matters of religion, art, literature, politics, and science. Their views were advanced, as befitted young men of high ideals and ability. Many of this group later rose to eminence in the great activities of England in the first half of the century.

We have some interesting accounts of how Tennyson appeared to others at this time and later — "like a poet," it was often said, but not pale and feeble. He was tall, broad-shouldered, powerful. His features were clear cut and strong, his hair dark and wavy. Later, when his fame brought him and Thomas Carlyle together, Carlyle wrote of him : " A fine, large featured, dim-eyed, bronze-coloured, shaggy-headed man is Alfred ; dusty, smoky, free and easy ; . . . a most restful, brotherly, solid-hearted man." And again : "One of the finest looking men in the world. A great shock of rough, dusky, dark hair ; bright, laughing hazel eyes ; massive, aquiline face, most massive yet most delicate ; of sallow brown complexion, almost Indian looking ; clothes cynically loose, free and easy, smokes infinite tobacco. His voice is musical, metallic, fit for loud laughter and piercing wail,

and all that may lie between ; speech and speculatio:
free and plenteous ; I do not meet in these late decade
such company over a pipe ! We shall see what he wil
grow to." When we remember that Carlyle liked ;
manly man, and that he knew one when he saw him.
we are set to wondering how some people— especially
boys —ever get the notion that a poet cannot be manly.
or that poetry is not made for manly readers. Both
Gladstone and Lincoln, the great statesmen who were
of Tennyson's own age, were lovers of poetry ; so
were the great scientists Huxley and Tyndall, the
former being among Tennyson's intimate friends.

Tennyson's first volume of verse, after his juvenile
work mentioned above, was *Poems, Chiefly Lyrical*,
issued in 1830. In 1832 appeared another volume, en-
titled simply *Poems*. In 1842 appeared his *English
Idylls*. Now between these last two volumes there is
a considerable interval, not only in time but in character. The poems of the first two volumes were light,
graceful, musical, but with only here and there an
expression of serious thought or deep purpose. They
were pretty, but without weight. In the 1842 volume,
however, it was at once apparent that here was a poet
who could not only see beauty, but think and feel
more deeply than other men — a man who was cast in
a larger mould. This growth in Tennyson is accounted
for in two ways. First, he had developed his powers
by study and thought, as he had changed from a boy
of twenty-three to a man of thirty-three. Second he
had had an experience that had set him to thinking
more deeply upon the great problems of life. This was
the death in 1833 of his dearest friend, Arthur Hallam ; the friend to whose memory was written the
great poem *In Memoriam*. So general and so cordial

as the reception given to the volume of 1842 that Tennyson's fame as a poet could now be considered established. From this time on to the end of his long life, he published new volumes of poetry at short intervals.

After leaving the university, Tennyson continued to study and write, setting himself, as Milton had done, seriously to the task of improving his knowledge and his powers. The ten years between 1832 and 1842 were a period of solitude and work. The death of Arthur Hallam had deeply saddened him. The death of his father about the same time not only brought sorrow to the family but lessened their income and made necessary their removal from their old home, the vicarage at Somersby. Yet so well spent were these years of sorrow and narrowed income that the poems he published in 1842 put Tennyson at once in the rank of England's great poets.

From this time on, both his name and his prosperity grew. In 1845 he was given by the Government a pension of two hundred pounds a year. He published in 1847 a long poem, *The Princess*, dealing in a half-serious, half-humorous way with the question of the education of women and their place in the world; and in 1850, *In Memoriam*, one of his greatest and most famous poems.

His eminence being now secure, and his revenue from the sale of his poetry sufficient, he married Emily Sellwood, to whom he had formerly been engaged. Shortly after his marriage he was made poet-laureate, succeeding in this honor a poet of no less distinction than the great Wordsworth, who had recently died. In 1853 he bought a house at Farringford on the Isle of Wight. Here he spent in study and retirement the most of the remaining forty years of his life. In 1868 he built himself a fine summer house at Aldworth, Surrey. But it is the Isle of Wight that we think of as the home of Tennyson.

The publication of *Maud* in 1855 and of *The Idylls of the King* (containing Enid, Vivien, Elaine, and Guinevere) in 1859 still further increased the poet's fame. Ten thousand copies of the *Idylls* were sold in the first six weeks. And though he published a number of poems in the succeeding thirty years, among them poems of such wide popularity as *Enoch Arden*, nothing could make his name better known. He was, by 1860, already regarded as England's foremost living poet.

Many honors came to him in the latter half of his life. Oxford University gave him an honorary degree. The University of Glasgow offered him the position of lord rector. In 1873 he declined a baronetcy; but when, in 1884, he was offered a peerage, he accepted it, as he said, for the sake of his elder son Hallam. Among his friends he numbered such men as Gladstone, Browning, Carlyle, Ruskin, Thackeray, Fitzgerald, and Huxley. To the end of his life he retained his faculties in full vigor. He died in October, 1892.

Like most great men Tennyson had many interests. All his life he was a reader, a student, and an observer; he knew not only literature, but history, politics, and science. He was in touch with all the important things that the men of his day were thinking and doing. He loved nature for its beauties, and he studied it as science. He traveled frequently, both in the British Islands and on the Continent, finding wild scenery such as that of the Pyrenees Mountains especially to his taste.

He was, for all his vigor, a shy and sensitive man, not seeking notoriety, shrinking under hostile criticism, quick to feel the rights or the sufferings of others. An essentially earnest man, he has filled his poetry with the more serious thoughts of his age. Religious faith, and its power to make men better; scientific doubt, and its power to free men from superstition; knowledge, and its power to make men strong and free; greed, and its tendency to make men base, cruel, and corrupt; ideals, and their power to lift men to higher planes of feeling and conduct; the eternal conflict of right and wrong; death and the future life; true patriotism, and its power to lift the country above cowardice and greed; the beauty of charity, of love, of the domestic affections; — these are the threads that run through all the beautifully wrought and fanciful fabric of his poetry. And so we find him both in his life and in his work, high-minded, thoughtful, and a lover of the beautiful.

THE ARTHURIAN LEGENDS

The Arthurian legends, the stories of King Arthur and his knights of the Round Table, have had a long and varied history. They were not made by any one man, or at any one place, or at any one time. They began somewhere back in the dim past, perhaps about the seventh century, as tales about a Celtic King Arthur, who had led the Britons in their battles against the heathen hordes of Saxon invaders, and, as the historian Nennius writing two centuries later tells us, "defeated them in twelve great battles." Whether Arthur was real, or the battles twelve, or anything certain, we shall never know; but scholars are now inclined to

Origin and development of the Arthurian myths

believe that there was a real King Arthur, a leader c
power enough to have his name taken up and passe
on in popular tradition, — not through written record
but by word of mouth.

The stories passed from land to land and from cen
tury to century through a stretch of eight hundre
years. When the Normans came over and conquere
England in the eleventh century, they found then
there as a survival of Celtic traditions about the
heroic past of the Celts. The stories then passed over
into France, and took the flavor of French chivalry
with its ideals of bravery, courtesy, and love. Then,
as they spread in France and Germany and England,
they absorbed the myths and legends of Christianity,
the customs and ideals of new centuries, and other
stories that were at first not even known to the original makers of the legends about Arthur. Such addi-
tions were, for example, the story of Lancelot, the
story of Tristan and Isolde, and the legend of the
Holy Grail.

Finally, these composite stories were gathered and
arranged into some sort of unity by Sir Thomas
Malory, and printed by Thomas Caxton, the first
English printer. A part of Caxton's introduction
shows how he regarded it : —

" And I, according to my copy, have down set it in
print, to the intent that noble men may see and learn
Malory's the noble acts of chivalry, the gentle and
Morte virtuous deeds that some knights used in
d'Arthur those days, by which they came to honor,
and how they that were vicious were punished, and
oft put to shame and rebuke. . . . For herein may
be seen noble chivalry, courtesy, humanity, friendli-
ness, hardiness, love, friendship, cowardice, murder,

ate, virtue, and sin. Do after the good, and leave
he evil, and it shall bring you unto good fame and
enown. And, for to pass the time, this book shall be
pleasant to read in, but for to give faith and belief
that all is true that is contained herein, ye be at your
own liberty."

So seemed these stories to a wise man of the fif-
teenth century; and so they seemed to Tennyson,
when he drew upon them for *The Idylls of the King*.

An outline of the history and development of these
legends is given as follows in Andrew Lang's *Tennyson*:[1] —

A sketch of the evolution of the Arthurian legends might
run thus: —

Sixth to eighth century, growth of myth about an Arthur,
real, or supposed to be real.

Tenth century, the Duchies of Normandy and Brittany
are in close relations; by the eleventh century Normans know Celtic Arthurian stories.

After 1066, Normans in contact with the Celtic peoples
of this island are in touch with the Arthur tales.

1130–1145, works on Arthurian matter by Geoffrey of
Monmouth.

1155, Wace's French translation of Geoffrey.

1150–1182, Chrétien de Troyes writes poems on Arthurian topics.

French prose romances on Arthur, from, say, 1180 to
1250. Those romances reach Wales, and modify, in
translations, the original Welsh legends, or, in part,
supplant them.

Amplifications and recastings are numerous. In 1485
Caxton publishes Malory's selections from French and
English sources, the whole being Tennyson's main
source, *Le Morte d'Arthur*.

[1] *Alfred Tennyson*, by Andrew Lang. Dodd, Mead and Company.
1901.

THE IDYLLS OF THE KING

Tennyson regarded the Arthur stories as the "most wonderful poetic material in the world." Nor was he the first English poet to feel their fascination. For a hundred years or more after Malory published his *Morte d'Arthur*, the book was popular, and the stories were often referred to in other literature. Spenser introduced them into *The Faerie Queene*, and both Milton and Dryden thought of making them the subject of an epic. Scott revived them in the nineteenth century, by introducing Arthur and Merlin into his poem, *The Bridal of Triermain*. Tennyson's interest in the stories dates from his boyhood. "The vision of Arthur as I have drawn him," he said, "had come upon me when, little more than a boy, I first lighted upon Malory." And the theme continued to interest him throughout his long life. In the 1832 volume, in *The Lady of Shalott*, he introduces the story of Elaine and her love for Lancelot. In the 1842 volume, *English Idylls*, there were three poems on Arthurian themes: the *Morte d'Arthur*, *Sir Galahad*, and *Sir Lancelot and Queen Guinevere*. And in the introduction to *Morte d'Arthur*, called *The Epic*, he speaks of the poem as the last of twelve books of an epic, which indeed it later came to be. It is clear, then, that Tennyson had in 1842 already come to think of the Arthurian stories as the material for an epic.

The *Idylls* were not produced as one great poem, but as a number of short poems, grouped around a central figure and a common topic, written at different times, and finally unified into one poem. Just what this means must be made a little clearer. All

(margin note: Tennyson's interest in the stories)

the *Idylls* draw their materials from the legends about Arthur and his knights of the Round Table; each of them gives some part of the Subject of the Idylls story of how Arthur founded his kingdom, how evil came into the court, how it spread, and how it finally resulted in the disruption of that " goodly fellowship," the defeat of Arthur's high purposes, and the overthrow of his kingdom. The *Idylls*, as finally arranged to develop this story, are as follows : —

The Coming of Arthur (1869)	Lancelot and Elaine (1859)
Gareth and Lynette (1872)	The Holy Grail (1869)
The Marriage of Geraint (1859)	Pelleas and Ettarre (1869)
	The Last Tournament (1872)
Geraint and Enid (1859)	Guinevere (1859)
Balin and Balan (1885)	The Passing of Arthur (1842,
Merlin and Vivien (1859)	1869)

A glance at the dates of the publication of these poems makes clear the point of Professor Van Dyke's comment that Tennyson " began with the end, continued with the beginning, and ended with the middle of the story."

What purpose, if any, had Tennyson beyond retelling these beautiful and romantic stories? From their first appearance they provoked Tennyson's purpose in the Idylls this question, a question which has ever since called forth various answers. The poet has himself spoken on the subject in no uncertain terms.

They have taken my hobby and ridden it too hard, and have explained some things too allegorically, although there is an allegorical, or perhaps rather a parabolic drift in the poem. . . .

Of course Camelot, for instance, a city of shadowy palaces, is everywhere symbolic of the gradual growth of human beliefs and institutions and of the spiritual develop-

ment of man. Yet there is no single fact or incident in the
Idylls, however seemingly mystical, which cannot be explained as without any mystery or allegory whatever.

Once, when asked whether those were right who
interpreted the three Queens who accompanied Arthur on his last voyage as Faith, Hope, and Charity,
he answered : —

They are right, and they are not right. They mean
that, and they do not. They are three of the noblest of
women. They are also those three Graces, but they are
much more. I hate to be tied down to say, " *This* means
that," because the thought within the image is much more
than any one interpretation.

In the same vein, Tennyson makes Percivale say,
at the end of his long story in *The Holy Grail :* —

So spake the King ; I know not all he meant.

So Merlin, when questioned about the mystery of
Arthur's origin, replies " in riddling triplets of old
time " : —

And truth is this to me, and that to thee ;
And truth or clothed or naked let it be.

When Gareth comes to Camelot (in *Gareth and
Lynette*), Merlin tells him, the city

is enchanted, son,
For there is nothing in it as it seems,
Saving the King ; tho' some there be that hold
The King a shadow, and the city real.

And yet, though he " hated to be tied down " to too
minute an explanation, Tennyson has put the epic
unity and the general meaning of the *Idylls* into ex-
plicit, though general, terms, in the *Dedication to the
Queen* at the end of the poem : —

> Accept this old imperfect tale,
> New-old, and shadowing Sense at war with Soul,
> Rather than that gray king, whose name, a ghost,
> Streams like a cloud, man-shaped, from mountain peak,
> And cleaves to cairn and cromlech still : or him
> Of Geoffrey's book, or him of Malleor's.

Here is the key to the meaning of the whole poem — "Sense at war with Soul " : the conflict between the lower and the higher, between evil and good. Here is the " parabolic significance " — the resemblance of the poem to a parable ; it illustrates in story form what goes on forever in the world at large and in the life of every one, the conflict between good and evil.

The key to the whole poem.

Arthur and his knights of the Round Table are seeking to establish a kingdom in which peace, safety, morality, and religion shall overcome disorder, cruelty, injustice, and all forms of wickedness. In the first two Idylls the good prevails. In the next two, the story of Geraint and Enid, evil has crept into the Court in the guilty love of Guinevere and Lancelot, and the rumor of this threatens the happiness of Geraint and Enid ; but in the end the good again prevails. In the next, *Balin and Balan*, we have the first tragic outcome of the sin at the Court : the rumor of it leads the two brothers to fight and kill each other. In *Merlin and Vivien*, the spirit of the Court has become poisoned by evil ; and from this time on the high purposes of Arthur are frustrated more and more by the spread of evil among those who should support him. In *Lancelot and Elaine* it is Lancelot's guilty love that keeps him from the pure love of Elaine, and causes the tragedy of her death. In *The Holy Grail* there is a sort of interlude in the moral dissolution of the Court. The knights go on a sacred quest ; but they neglect their higher duties, their loyalty to the great work of the King, and all but two or three of them, failing to see the Grail because they are not pure in heart, have, as Arthur says, "followed wandering fires." In *Guinevere*, the next to the last, the guilt of Lancelot and the Queen is made clear even to the unsuspicious King, the Queen flees to a convent, and Lancelot and the disloyal knights array themselves in civil war against the King. In *The Passing of Arthur* we have the end of the cycle, the complete overthrow of Arthur's reign of peace and goodness.

Is the ending hopeless? Not quite. Arthur may come again, and reëstablish his power. Even though he may not come, there are to be other ways, other systems, to accomplish good and defeat evil.

> The old order changeth, yielding place to new,
> And God fulfils himself in many ways,
> Lest one good custom should corrupt the world.

This is a recurrent idea in Tennyson's work. In *In Memoriam* he wrote, —

> Our little systems have their day,
> They have their day and cease to be ;
> They are but broken parts of Thee,
> And Thou, O Lord, art more than they.

So much for the general meaning of *The Idylls*. There are other ideas included in them. In *Gareth and Lynette* there is a clear allegory, interpreted by the poet as "the war of time against the soul of man," and reflecting the general teaching of the whole series. The characters represent types : "Lancelot, the noblest brother and the truest man," with the good unconquered in him even by his

Other meanings

sin; " Tristram the bold and careless hunter, Galahad the pure, unearthly knight, Bors the blunt and honest, Bedivere the warm-hearted." Arthur is a type of perfection, and perhaps for that reason rather cold and unreal.

In *Gareth and Lynette* we have the ideals of King Arthur's court at their point of highest influence. Evil and violence still exist in the land, but the Knights of the Round Table are overcoming them in combat and by their own high standards of conduct. The conflict between " Sense and Soul," that is, between the lower and the higher things, is in part a conflict of ideals: between Gareth and his mother; between Gareth and Lynette, who judges him by externals, but is in the end constrained to recognize true knighthood apart from rank; within Gareth himself, who cheerfully accepts social humiliation for the opportunity to achieve higher things. In every aspect of this story the good triumphs; it is a victory of Soul over Sense.

In *Lancelot and Elaine* the evil at the Court is growing. The Queen's guilty love has an indirect influence for harm to others. It causes the death of Elaine, and leaves in us a foreboding of further evil and sorrow. This Idyll is less allegorical than *Gareth and Lynette*. In spite of its extreme romanticism, it is a story of human beings, rather than a parable for the illustration of some general truth. In the progress of the struggle of Sense and Soul it stands as a sort of crisis or turning-point, with the evil in the ascendancy.

A manuscript note by the poet runs : —

The coming of Arthur is on the night of the New Year; when he is wedded " the world is white with May "; on a summer night the vision of the Holy Grail appears; and

the Last Tournament is in the "yellowing Autumn-tide."
Guinevere flees thro' the mists of autumn, and Arthur's
death takes place at midnight in midwinter.

Can the reader do better than accept Tennyson's
own meaning and purpose in *The Idylls?* To find in
them nothing more than a series of beautiful pictures
in romantic colors is something, but it is not enough;
to twist them into minute and definite allegorical
meanings is too much. They were writtten to charm
us by their beauty, by their appeal to our imagina-
tions ; and, in addition, to inculcate certain high ideals
of life.

The term " Idylls " was deliberately chosen by Tennyson to designate the nature of the poem: not an

**The name
"Idylls"** epic in the ordinary sense of a long, detailed
and sustained story, but a succession of
shorter stories, idylls (from the Greek *eidyllion*, meaning a little picture), united by a common thread of
theme and purpose into a unified whole.

The diction is appropriate to the theme. It is digni-
fied, formal, archaic. Rare words are used sometimes

Diction to designate unfamiliar things, sometimes to
impart the flavor of antiquity that belongs
to these old stories. Many figurative expressions are
used. A random glance over the pages shows many
such : A doubt that ever smouldered ; like a painted
battle the war stood ; a voice as of the waters ; Rome,
slow-fading mistress of the world ; heapt in mounds
and ridges all the sea drove like a cataract ; his own
thought drove him like a goad ; brightening the skirts
of a long cloud ; a cry that shivered to the tingling
stars ; so the whole round earth is every way bound
by gold chains about the feet of God. In such figurative passages, and in brilliant, highly colored pictures

the pages of Tennyson abound. In a very real sense
he is one of the most " picturesque " of our poets.

The verse is, except in the lyrics now and then
introduced, pentameter blank verse. This **The verse-
forms** means unrhymed verse, with five beats or
accents to a line. Thus: —

> So all day long the noise of battle rolled
> Among the mountains by the winter sea.
>
> So saying, from the ruined shrine he stept,
> And in the moon athwart the place of tombs,
> Where lay the mighty bones of ancient men,
> Old knights, and over them the sea-wind sang
> Shrill, chill, with flakes of foam. He stepping down
> By zig-zag paths, and juts of pointed rock,
> Came on the shining levels of the lake.

But good verse is not to be read with the beats or
accents evenly strong. In the first line above, " So all
day long," etc., the stresses are nearly equal. In the
next line they are by no means so: the word *by* has
almost no stress. So in the first line of the next passage, *from* is not stressed; in the second line, *in* is
not; and in the last line, *on* is but faintly accented
and *of* not at all. Now note what is gained by these
variations. Each of these unstressed or faintly stressed
syllables either follows or precedes a foot (of two
syllables) in which the stress is very strong. Sometimes the stress may be equally distributed on the two
syllables of a foot, as in the sixth, the seventh, and
the last line above. We may even have the order re-
versed, for the sake of variety, and have the stress fall

on the first syllable of the foot, making a *trochee* instead of an *iambus*, thus : —

> Wearing the white flower of a blameless life.

If we indicate the faint or absent accent by a single mark, and the strong accent by a double mark, these variations are more clearly seen.

> Among the mountains by the winter sea.

> And in the moon athwart the place of tombs.

> Came on the shining levels of the lake.

> Torn as a sail that leaves the rope is torn.

These changes in stress give a pleasing variety to the verse : they break up the monotony of sound ; so that the rhythm is very different from the mechanical effect of a Mother Goose rhyme : —

> Hickory, dickory, dock,

> The mouse ran up the clock,

> The clock struck one,

> The mouse ran down,

> Hickory, dickory, dock.

But there is another advantage in this variation of stress. The accent is taken off the unimportant words, and falls, therefore, the more heavily on the important words. Thus they are made to stand out, not only by their meaning, but by their sound. Test any passage in these poems, and you will find this to be true.

What should a high school student make of these poems ? He need hardly expect to see in them as yet all that Tennyson meant, or all that trained minds of older people see. If he derives pleasure from the use of his imagination and of his thinking powers, and if he is willing to

On the reading of Tennyson

take the pains to read carefully and thoughtfully, he may fairly expect to find in reading them an ample reward in pleasure of a high order. If he is unwilling to use his mind, he cannot expect to get much pleasure out of his reading, either in this book or in most others that belong to what is called good literature. The great poets and prose writers have not written for the sluggish reader; they have preferred to address a more deserving audience. Are they not justified?

Tennyson is a poet for the young as well as for the old. He has given deep pleasure to thousands of boys and girls in their "teens." The way to acquire such pleasure in poetry is to read poetry; the way to increase it is to read more poetry. It would be well for readers of this volume to extend their knowledge of the *Idylls* by reading also, *Geraint and Enid*, *The Holy Grail*, and *Guinevere*. These are not hard reading, and they are full of beautiful passages. A list of the other good things in Tennyson would be too long to give. But here is a partial list, chosen for beauty and simplicity : —

Mariana
The Lady of Shalott
The Miller's Daughter
Lady Clara Vere de Vere
The Lotos Eaters
Choric Song
Dora
The Talking Oak
Ulysses
The Day Dream
Sir Galahad
Lady Clare

The Eagle
Break, break, break
The Charge of the Light
  Brigade
Enoch Arden
The Revenge
The Defence of Lucknow
The Northern Farmer
The Spinster's Sweet-'Arts
Owd Röa
Merlin and the Gleam
Crossing the Bar

A BIBLIOGRAPHY

THE ARTHURIAN LEGENDS

Elsdale, Henry. *Studies in the Idylls.*
Lang, Andrew. *Tennyson.*
Lawrence, W. W. *Medieval Stories.*
Littledale, Harold. *Studies in the Idylls.*
Maccallum, M. W. *Tennyson's Idylls.*
Rhys, John. *Studies in the Arthurian Legend.*

LIFE OF TENNYSON

Cary, E. L. *Tennyson, His Homes,* etc.
Hinchman and Gummere. *Lives of Great Writers.*
Lang, Andrew. *Tennyson.*
Lyall, Herbert. *Tennyson.*
Stephen, Leslie. *Studies of a Biographer,* vol. II.
Tennyson, Hallam. *Memoirs of Tennyson.*
Walters, J. C. *In Tennyson Land.*
Waugh, Arthur. *Alfred, Lord Tennyson.*
World's Best Literature. Article on Tennyson, vol. XXIV.

CRITICISM OF TENNYSON

Brooke, Stopford A. *Tennyson, His Art,* etc.
Chesterton, G. K. *Varied Types.*
Dowden, Edward. *Studies in Literature.*
Gates, W. E. *Studies and Appreciations.*
Harrison, Frederic. *Tennyson and Other Literary Estimates.*
Hutton, R. H. *Essays, Literary.*
James, Henry. *Views and Reviews.*
Noel, Roden. *Essays on Poetry and Poets.*
Paul, Herbert. *Men and Letters.*
Saintsbury, G. E. *Corrected Impressions.*
Van Dyke, Henry. *The Poetry of Tennyson.*

IDYLLS OF THE KING

IN TWELVE BOOKS

Flos Regum Arthurus. — JOSEPH OF EXETER.

DEDICATION

THESE to His Memory — since he held them dear,
Perchance as finding there unconsciously
Some image of himself — I dedicate,
I dedicate, I consecrate with tears —
These Idylls.

          And indeed He seems to me   5
Scarce other than my king's ideal knight,
" Who reverenced his conscience as his king ;
Whose glory was, redressing human wrong ;
Who spake no slander, no, nor listen'd to it ;
Who loved one only and who clave to her — "   10
Her — over all whose realms to their last isle,
Commingled with the gloom of imminent war,
The shadow of His loss drew like eclipse,
Darkening the world. We have lost him : he is gone :
We know him now : all narrow jealousies   15
Are silent ; and we see him as he moved,
How modest, kindly, all-accomplish'd, wise,
With what sublime repression of himself,
And in what limits, and how tenderly ;
Not swaying to this faction or to that ;   20
Not making his high place the lawless perch
Of wing'd ambitions, nor a vantage-ground

For pleasure; but thro' all this tract of years
Wearing the white flower of a blameless life,
Before a thousand peering littlenesses,   25
In that fierce light which beats upon a throne,
And blackens every blot: for where is he,
Who dares foreshadow for an only son
A lovelier life, a more unstain'd than his?
Or how should England dreaming of *his* sons   30
Hope more for these than some inheritance
Of such a life, a heart, a mind as thine,
Thou noble Father of her Kings to be,
Laborious for her people and her poor —
Voice in the rich dawn of an ampler day —   35
Far-sighted summoner of War and Waste
To fruitful strifes and rivalries of peace —
Sweet nature gilded by the gracious gleam
Of letters, dear to Science, dear to Art,
Dear to thy land and ours, a Prince indeed,   40
Beyond all titles, and a household name,
Hereafter, thro' all times, Albert the Good.

Break not, O woman's-heart, but still endure;
Break not, for thou art Royal, but endure,
Remembering all the beauty of that star   45
Which shone so close beside Thee that ye made
One light together, but has past and leaves
The Crown a lonely splendor.

                    May all love,
His love, unseen but felt, o'ershadow Thee,
The love of all Thy sons encompass Thee,   50
The love of all Thy daughters cherish Thee,
The love of all Thy people comfort Thee,
Till God's love set Thee at his side again!

THE COMING OF ARTHUR

LEODOGRAN, the King of Cameliard,
Had one fair daughter, and none other child ;
And she was fairest of all flesh on earth,
Guinevere, and in her his one delight.

For many a petty king ere Arthur came   5
Ruled in this isle, and ever waging war
Each upon other, wasted all the land ;
And still from time to time the heathen host
Swarm'd overseas, and harried what was left.
And so there grew great tracts of wilderness,   10
Wherein the beast was ever more and more,
But man was less and less, till Arthur came.
For first Aurelius lived and fought and died,
And after him King Uther fought and died,
But either fail'd to make the kingdom one.   15
And after these King Arthur for a space,
And thro' the puissance of his Table Round,
Drew all their petty princedoms under him,
Their king and head, and made a realm, and reign'd.

And thus the land of Cameliard was waste,   20
Thick with wet woods, and many a beast therein,
And none or few to scare or chase the beast ;
So that wild dog, and wolf and boar and bear
Came night and day, and rooted in the fields,
And wallow'd in the gardens of the King.   25
And ever and anon the wolf would steal
The children and devour, but now and then,
Her own brood lost or dead, lent her first teat

To human sucklings; and the children, housed
In her foul den, there at their meat would growl,   30
And mock their foster-mother on four feet,
Till, straighten'd, they grew up to wolf-like men,
Worse than the wolves. And King Leodogran
Groan'd for the Roman legions here again,
And Cæsar's eagle: then his brother king,   35
Urien, assail'd him: last a heathen horde,
Reddening the sun with smoke and earth with blood,
And on the spike that split the mother's heart
Spitting the child, brake on him, till, amazed,
He knew not whither he should turn for aid.   40

But — for he heard of Arthur newly crown'd,
Tho' not without an uproar made by those
Who cried, " He is not Uther's son " — the King
Sent to him, saying, " Arise, and help us thou !
For here between the man and beast we die."   45

And Arthur yet had done no deed of arms,
But heard the call, and came : and Guinevere
Stood by the castle walls to watch him pass ;
But since he neither wore on helm or shield
The golden symbol of his kinglihood,   50
But rode a simple knight among his knights,
And many of these in richer arms than he,
She saw him not, or mark'd not, if she saw,
One among many, tho' his face was bare.
But Arthur, looking downward as he past,   55
Felt the light of her eyes into his life
Smite on the sudden, yet rode on, and pitch'd
His tents beside the forest. Then he drave
The heathen ; after, slew the beast, and fell'd
The forest, letting in the sun, and made   60

Broad pathways for the hunter and the knight
And so return'd.

        For while he linger'd there,
A doubt that ever smoulder'd in the hearts
Of those great Lords and Barons of his realm
Flash'd forth and into war: for most of these,   65
Colleaguing with a score of petty kings,
Made head against him, crying, "Who is he
That he should rule us? who hath proven him
King Uther's son? for lo! we look at him,
And find nor face nor bearing, limbs nor voice,   70
Are like to those of Uther whom we knew.
This is the son of Gorloïs, not the King;
This is the son of Anton, not the King."

    And Arthur, passing thence to battle, felt
Travail, and throes and agonies of the life,   75
Desiring to be join'd with Guinevere;
And thinking as he rode, "Her father said
That there between the man and beast they die.
Shall I not lift her from this land of beasts
Up to my throne, and side by side with me?   80
What happiness to reign a lonely king,
Vext — O ye stars that shudder over me,
O earth that soundest hollow under me,
Vext with waste dreams? for saving I be join'd
To her that is the fairest under heaven,   85
I seem as nothing in the mighty world,
And cannot will my will, nor work my work
Wholly, nor make myself in mine own realm
Victor and lord. But were I join'd with her,
Then might we live together as one life,   90
And reigning with one will in everything

Have power on this dark land to lighten it,
And power on this dead world to make it live."

    Thereafter — as he speaks who tells the tale —
When Arthur reach'd a field-of-battle bright   95
With pitch'd pavilions of his foe, the world
Was all so clear about him, that he saw
The smallest rock far on the faintest hill,
And even in high day the morning star.
So when the King had set his banner broad,   100
At once from either side, with trumpet-blast,
And shouts, and clarions shrilling unto blood,
The long-lanced battle let their horses run.
And now the Barons and the kings prevail'd,
And now the King, as here and there that war   105
Went swaying; but the Powers who walk the world
Made lightnings and great thunders over him,
And dazed all eyes, till Arthur by main might,
And mightier of his hands with every blow,
And leading all his knighthood threw the kings   110
Carádos, Urien, Cradlemont of Wales,
Claudius, and Clariance of Northumberland,
The King Brandagoras of Latangor,
With Anguisant of Erin, Morganore,
And Lot of Orkney. Then, before a voice   115
As dreadful as the shout of one who sees
To one who sins, and deems himself alone
And all the world asleep, they swerved and brake
Flying, and Arthur call'd to stay the brands
That hack'd among the flyers, " Ho! they yield!"   120
So like a painted battle the war stood
Silenced, the living quiet as the dead,
And in the heart of Arthur joy was lord.
He laugh'd upon his warrior whom he loved

And honor'd most. "Thou dost not doubt me King, 125
So well thine arm hath wrought for me to-day."
"Sir and my liege," he cried, "the fire of God
Descends upon thee in the battle-field:
I know thee for my King!" Whereat the two,
For each had warded either in the fight,   130
Sware on the field of death a deathless love,
And Arthur said, "Man's word is God in man:
Let chance what will, I trust thee to the death."

Then quickly from the foughten field he sent
Ulfius, and Brastias, and Bedivere,   135
His new-made knights, to King Leodogran,
Saying, "If I in aught have served thee well,
Give me thy daughter Guinevere to wife."

Whom when he heard, Leodogran in heart
Debating — "How should I that am a king,   140
However much he help me at my need,
Give my one daughter saving to a king,
And a king's son?" — lifted his voice, and call'd
A hoary man, his chamberlain, to whom
He trusted all things, and of him required   145
His counsel: "Knowest thou aught of Arthur's
      birth?"

Then spake the hoary chamberlain and said,
"Sir King, there be but two old men that know:
And each is twice as old as I; and one
Is Merlin, the wise man that ever served   150
King Uther thro' his magic art; and one
Is Merlin's master (so they call him) Bleys,
Who taught him magic; but the scholar ran
Before the master, and so far, that Bleys

Laid magic by, and sat him down, and wrote   155
All things and whatsoever Merlin did
In one great annal-book, where after-years
Will learn the secret of our Arthur's birth."

To whom the King Leodogran replied,
"O friend, had I been holpen half as well   160
By this King Arthur as by thee to-day,
Then beast and man had had their share of me:
But summon here before us yet once more
Ulfius, and Brastias, and Bedivere."

Then, when they came before him, the King said, 165
"I have seen the cuckoo chased by lesser fowl,
And reason in the chase: but wherefore now
Do these your lords stir up the heat of war,
Some calling Arthur born of Gorloïs,
Others of Anton? Tell me, ye yourselves,   170
Hold ye this Arthur for King Uther's son?"

And Ulfius and Brastias answer'd, "Ay."
Then Bedivere, the first of all his knights
Knighted by Arthur at his crowning, spake —
For bold in heart and act and word was he,   175
Whenever slander breathed against the King —

"Sir, there be many rumors on this head:
For there be those who hate him in their hearts,
Call him baseborn, and since his ways are sweet,
And theirs are bestial, hold him less than man: 180
And there be those who deem him more than man,
And dream he dropt from heaven: but my belief
In all this matter — so ye care to learn —
Sir, for ye know that in King Uther's time

The prince and warrior Gorloïs, he that held 185
Tintagil castle by the Cornish sea,
Was wedded with a winsome wife, Ygerne:
And daughters had she borne him, — one whereof,
Lot's wife, the Queen of Orkney, Bellicent,
Hath ever like a loyal sister cleaved 190
To Arthur, — but a son she had not borne.
And Uther cast upon her eyes of love:
But she, a stainless wife to Gorloïs,
So loathed the bright dishonor of his love,
That Gorloïs and King Uther went to war: 195
And overthrown was Gorloïs and slain.
Then Uther in his wrath and heat besieged
Ygerne within Tintagil, where her men,
Seeing the mighty swarm about their walls,
Left her and fled, and Uther enter'd in, 200
And there was none to call to but himself.
So, compass'd by the power of the King,
Enforced she was to wed him in her tears,
And with a shameful swiftness: afterward,
Not many moons, King Uther died himself, 205
Moaning and wailing for an heir to rule
After him, lest the realm should go to wrack.
And that same night, the night of the new year,
By reason of the bitterness and grief
That vext his mother, all before his time 210
Was Arthur born, and all as soon as born
Deliver'd at a secret postern-gate
To Merlin, to be holden far apart
Until his hour should come; because the lords
Of that fierce day were as the lords of this, 215
Wild beasts, and surely would have torn the child
Piecemeal among them, had they known; for each
But sought to rule for his own self and hand,

And many hated Uther for the sake
Of Gorloïs. Wherefore Merlin took the child,   220
And gave him to Sir Anton, an old knight
An ancient friend of Uther; and his wife
Nursed the young prince, and rear'd him with her own;
And no man knew. And ever since the lords
Have foughten like wild beasts among themselves, 225
So that the realm has gone to wrack: but now,
This year, when Merlin (for his hour had come)
Brought Arthur forth, and set him in the hall,
Proclaiming, 'Here is Uther's heir, your king,'
A hundred voices cried, 'Away with him!   230
No king of ours! a son of Gorloïs he,
Or else the child of Anton, and no king,
Or else baseborn.' Yet Merlin thro' his craft,
And while the people clamor'd for a king,
Had Arthur crown'd; but after, the great lords   235
Banded, and so brake out in open war."

Then while the King debated with himself
If Arthur were the child of shamefulness,
Or born the son of Gorloïs, after death,
Or Uther's son, and born before his time,   240
Or whether there were truth in anything
Said by these three, there came to Cameliard,
With Gawain and young Modred, her two sons,
Lot's wife, the Queen of Orkney, Bellicent;
Whom as he could, not as he would, the King   245
Made feast for, saying, as they sat at meat,

"A doubtful throne is ice on summer seas.
Ye come from Arthur's court. Victor his men
Report him! Yea, but ye — think ye this king —
So many those that hate him, and so strong,   250

So few his knights, however brave they be —
Hath body enow to hold his foemen down?"

"O King," she cried, "and I will tell thee: few,
Few, but all brave, all of one mind with him;
For I was near him when the savage yells   255
Of Uther's peerage died, and Arthur sat
Crown'd on the daïs, and his warriors cried,
'Be thou the king, and we will work thy will
Who love thee.' Then the King in low deep tones,
And simple words of great authority,   260
Bound them by so strait vows to his own self,
That when they rose, knighted from kneeling, some
Were pale as at the passing of a ghost,
Some flush'd, and others dazed, as one who wakes
Half-blinded at the coming of a light.   265

"But when he spake and cheer'd his Table Round
With large, divine, and comfortable words,
Beyond my tongue to tell thee — I beheld
From eye to eye thro' all their Order flash
A momentary likeness of the King: 270
And ere it left their faces, thro' the cross
And those around it and the Crucified,
Down from the casement over Arthur, smote
Flame-color, vert and azure, in three rays,
One falling upon each of three fair queens,   275
Who stood in silence near his throne, the friends
Of Arthur, gazing on him, tall, with bright
Sweet faces, who will help him at his need.

"And there I saw mage Merlin, whose vast wit
And hundred winters are but as the hands   280
Of loyal vassals toiling for their liege.

"And near him stood the Lady of the Lake,
Who knows a subtler magic than his own —
Clothed in white samite, mystic, wonderful.
She gave the King his huge cross-hilted sword,   285
Whereby to drive the heathen out: a mist
Of incense curl'd about her, and her face
Wellnigh was hidden in the minster gloom;
But there was heard among the holy hymns
A voice as of the waters, for she dwells   290
Down in a deep; calm, whatsoever storms
May shake the world, and when the surface rolls,
Hath power to walk the waters like our Lord.

"There likewise I beheld Excalibur
Before him at his crowning borne, the sword   295
That rose from out the bosom of the lake,
And Arthur row'd across and took it — rich
With jewels, elfin Urim, on the hilt,
Bewildering heart and eye — the blade so bright
That men are blinded by it — on one side,   300
Graven in the oldest tongue of all this world,
'Take me,' but turn the blade and ye shall see,
And written in the speech ye speak yourself,
'Cast me away!' And sad was Arthur's face
Taking it, but old Merlin counsell'd him,   305
'Take thou and strike! the time to cast away
Is yet far-off.' So this great brand the king
Took, and by this will beat his foemen down."

Thereat Leodogran rejoiced, but thought
To sift his doubtings to the last, and ask'd,   310
Fixing full eyes of question on her face,
"The swallow and the swift are near akin,
But thou art closer to this noble prince,

Being his own dear sister" ; and she said,
" Daughter of Gorloïs and Ygerne am I" ;   315
" And therefore Arthur's sister? " ask'd the King.
She answer'd, " These be secret things," and sign'd
To those two sons to pass and let them be.
And Gawain went, and breaking into song
Sprang out, and follow'd by his flying hair   320
Ran like a colt, and leapt at all he saw :
But Modred laid his ear beside the doors,
And there half-heard ; the same that afterward
Struck for the throne, and striking found his doom.

And then the Queen made answer, " What know I ?
For dark my mother was in eyes and hair,   326
And dark in hair and eyes am I ; and dark
Was Gorloïs, yea and dark was Uther too,
Wellnigh to blackness ; but this King is fair
Beyond the race of Britons and of men.   330
Moreover, always in my mind I hear
A cry from out the dawning of my life,
A mother weeping, and I hear her say,
'O that ye had some brother, pretty one,
To guard thee on the rough ways of the world.' "   335

" Ay," said the King, " and hear ye such a cry ?
But when did Arthur chance upon thee first? "

"O King ! " she cried, " and I will tell thee true :
He found me first when yet a little maid :
Beaten I had been for a little fault   340
Whereof I was not guilty ; and out I ran
And flung myself down on a bank of heath,
And hated this fair world and all therein,
And wept, and wish'd that I were dead ; and he —

I know not whether of himself he came,   345
Or brought by Merlin, who, they say, can walk
Unseen at pleasure — he was at my side,
And spake sweet words, and comforted my heart,
And dried my tears, being a child with me.
And many a time he came, and evermore   350
As I grew greater grew with me; and sad
At times he seem'd, and sad with him was I,
Stern too at times, and then I loved him not,
But sweet again, and then I loved him well.
And now of late I see him less and less,   355
But those first days had golden hours for me,
For then I surely thought he would be king.

  "But let me tell thee now another tale:
For Bleys, our Merlin's master, as they say,
Died but of late, and sent his cry to me,   360
To hear him speak before he left his life.
Shrunk like a fairy changeling lay the mage;
And when I enter'd told me that himself
And Merlin ever served about the King,
Uther, before he died; and on the night   365
When Uther in Tintagil past away
Moaning and wailing for an heir, the two
Left the still King, and passing forth to breathe,
Then from the castle gateway by the chasm
Descending thro' the dismal night — a night   370
In which the bounds of heaven and earth were lost —
Beheld, so high upon the dreary deeps
It seem'd in heaven, a ship, the shape thereof
A dragon wing'd, and all from stem to stern
Bright with a shining people on the decks,   375
And gone as soon as seen. And then the two
Dropt to the cove, and watch'd the great sea fall,

Wave after wave, each mightier than the last,
Till last, a ninth one, gathering half the deep
And full of voices, slowly rose and plunged   380
Roaring, and all the wave was in a flame:
And down the wave and in the flame was borne
A naked babe, and rode to Merlin's feet,
Who stoopt and caught the babe, and cried 'The
          King!
Here is an heir for Uther!' And the fringe   385
Of that great breaker, sweeping up the strand,
Lash'd at the wizard as he spake the word,
And all at once all round him rose in fire,
So that the child and he were clothed in fire.
And presently thereafter follow'd calm,   390
Free sky and stars: 'And this same child,' he said,
'Is he who reigns; nor could I part in peace
Till this were told.' And saying this the seer
Went thro' the strait and dreadful pass of death,
Not ever to be question'd any more   395
Save on the further side; but when I met
Merlin, and ask'd him if these things were truth —
The shining dragon and the naked child
Descending in the glory of the seas —
He laugh'd as is his wont, and answer'd me   400
In riddling triplets of old time, and said:

          "'Rain, rain, and sun! a rainbow in the sky!
A young man will be wiser by and by;
An old man's wit may wander ere he die.

          "'Rain, rain, and sun! a rainbow on the lea!   405
And truth is this to me, and that to thee;
And truth or clothed or naked let it be.

" ' Rain, sun, and rain! and the free blossom blows :
Sun, rain, and sun! and where is he who knows?
From the great deep to the great deep he goes.'   410

" So Merlin riddling anger'd me ; but thou
Fear not to give this King thine only child,
Guinevere : so great bards of him will sing
Hereafter ; and dark sayings from of old
Ranging and ringing thro' the minds of men,   415
And echo'd by old folk beside their fires
For comfort after their wage-work is done,
Speak of the King ; and Merlin in our time
Hath spoken also, not in jest, and sworn
Tho' men may wound him that he will not die,   420
But pass, again to come ; and then or now
Utterly smite the heathen underfoot,
Till these and all men hail him for their king."

She spake and King Leodogran rejoiced,
But musing "Shall I answer yea or nay?"   425
Doubted, and drowsed, nodded and slept, and saw,
Dreaming, a slope of land that ever grew,
Field after field, up to a height, the peak
Haze-hidden, and thereon a phantom king,
Now looming, and now lost ; and on the slope   430
The sword rose, the hind fell, the herd was driven,
Fire glimpsed ; and all the land from roof and rick,
In drifts of smoke before a rolling wind,
Stream'd to the peak, and mingled with the haze
And made it thicker ; while the phantom king   435
Sent out at times a voice ; and here or there
Stood one who pointed toward the voice, the rest
Slew on and burnt, crying, " No king of ours.
No son of Uther, and no king of ours " ;

Till with a wink his dream was changed, the haze 440
Descended, and the solid earth became
As nothing, but the King stood out in heaven,
Crown'd. And Leodogran awoke, and sent
Ulfius, and Brastias, and Bedivere
Back to the court of Arthur answering yea. 445

Then Arthur charged his warrior whom he loved
And honor'd most, Sir Lancelot, to ride forth
And bring the Queen ; — and watch'd him from the
    gates :
And Lancelot past away among the flowers,
(For then was latter April) and return'd 450
Among the flowers, in May, with Guinevere.
To whom arrived, by Dubric the high saint,
Chief of the church in Britain, and before
The stateliest of her altar-shrines, the King
That morn was married, while in stainless white, 455
The fair beginners of a nobler time,
And glorying in their vows and him, his knights
Stood round him, and rejoicing in his joy.
Far shone the fields of May thro' open door,
The sacred altar blossom'd white with May, 460
The Sun of May descended on their King,
They gazed on all earth's beauty in their Queen,
Roll'd incense, and there past along the hymns
A voice as of the waters, while the two
Sware at the shrine of Christ a deathless love : 465
And Arthur said, " Behold, thy doom is mine.
Let chance what will, I love thee to the death ! "
To whom the Queen replied with drooping eyes,
" King and my lord, I love thee to the death ! "
And holy Dubric spread his hands and spake, 470
" Reign ye, and live and love, and make the world

Other, and may thy Queen be one with thee,
And all this Order of thy Table Round
Fulfil the boundless purpose of their King!"

So Dubric said; but when they left the shrine 475
Great Lords from Rome before the portal stood,
In scornful stillness gazing as they past;
Then while they paced a city all on fire
With sun and cloth of gold, the trumpets blew,
And Arthur's knighthood sang before the King:— 480

" Blow trumpet, for the world is white with May;
Blow trumpet, the long night hath roll'd away!
Blow thro' the living world — ' Let the King reign.'

" Shall Rome or Heathen rule in Arthur's realm?
Flash brand and lance, fall battleaxe upon helm, 485
Fall battleaxe, and flash brand! Let the King reign.

"Strike for the King and live! his knights have heard
That God hath told the King a secret word.
Fall battleaxe, and flash brand! Let the King reign.

" Blow trumpet! he will lift us from the dust. 490
Blow trumpet! live the strength and die the lust!
Clang battleaxe, and clash brand! Let the King reign.

" Strike for the King and die! and if thou diest,
The King is King, and ever wills the highest.
Clang battleaxe, and clash brand! Let the King reign.

" Blow, for our Sun is mighty in his May! 496
Blow, for our Sun is mightier day by day!
Clang battleaxe, and clash brand! Let the King reign.

" The King will follow Christ, and we the King
In whom high God hath breathed a secret thing. 500
Fall battleaxe, and flash brand ! Let the King reign."

So sang the knighthood, moving to their hall.
There at the banquet those great Lords from Rome,
The slow-fading mistress of the world,
Strode in, and claim'd their tribute as of yore. 505
But Arthur spake, " Behold, for these have sworn
To wage my wars, and worship me their King;
The old order changeth, yielding place to new;
And we that fight for our fair father Christ,
Seeing that ye be grown too weak and old 510
To drive the heathen from your Roman wall,
No tribute will we pay " : so those great lords
Drew back in wrath, and Arthur strove with Rome.

And Arthur and his knighthood for a space
Were all one will, and thro' that strength the King 515
Drew in the petty princedoms under him,
Fought, and in twelve great battles overcame
The heathen hordes, and made a realm and reign'd.

GARETH AND LYNETTE

THE last tall son of Lot and Bellicent,
And tallest, Gareth, in a showerful spring
Stared at the spate. A slender-shafted pine
Lost footing, fell, and so was whirl'd away.
"How he went down," said Gareth, "as a false knight 5
Or evil king before my lance, if lance
Were mine to use — O senseless cataract,
Bearing all down in thy precipitancy —
And yet thou art but swollen with cold snows
And mine is living blood: thou dost His will, 10
The Maker's, and not knowest, and I that know,
Have strength and wit, in my good mother's hall
Linger with vacillating obedience,
Prison'd, and kept and coax'd and whistled to —
Since the good mother holds me still a child! 15
Good mother is bad mother unto me!
A worse were better; yet no worse would I.
Heaven yield her for it, but in me put force
To weary her ears with one continuous prayer,
Until she let me fly discaged to sweep 20
In ever-highering eagle-circles up
To the great Sun of Glory, and thence swoop
Down upon all things base, and dash them dead,
A knight of Arthur, working out his will,
To cleanse the world. Why, Gawain, when he came 25
With Modred hither in the summer-time,
Ask'd me to tilt with him, the proven knight.
Modred for want of worthier was the judge.
Then I so shook him in the saddle, he said,
'Thou hast half prevail'd against me,' said so — he — 30

Tho' Modred biting his thin lips was mute,
For he is alway sullen: what care I?"

And Gareth went, and hovering round her chair
Ask'd, "Mother, tho' ye count me still the child,
Sweet mother do ye love the child?" She laugh'd, 35
"Thou art but a wild-goose to question it."
"Then, mother, an ye love the child," he said,
"Being a goose, and rather tame than wild,
Hear the child's story." "Yea, my well-beloved,
An 't were but of the goose and golden eggs." 40

And Gareth answer'd her with kindling eyes:
"Nay, nay, good mother, but this egg of mine
Was finer gold than any goose can lay;
For this an eagle, a royal eagle, laid
Almost beyond eye-reach, on such a palm 45
As glitters gilded in thy Book of Hours.
And there was ever haunting round the palm
A lusty youth, but poor, who often saw
The splendor sparkling from aloft, and thought,
'An I could climb and lay my hand upon it, 50
Then were I wealthier than a leash of kings.'
But ever when he reach'd a hand to climb,
One that had loved him from his childhood caught
And stay'd him, 'Climb not lest thou break thy neck,
I charge thee by my love,' and so the boy, 55
Sweet mother, neither clomb nor brake his neck,
But brake his very heart in pining for it,
And past away."

To whom the mother said,
"True love, sweet son, had risk'd himself and climb'd,
And handed down the golden treasure to him." 60

And Gareth answer'd her with kindling eyes:
" Gold? said I gold?— ay then, why he, or she,
Or whosoe'er it was, or half the world
Had ventured — *had* the thing I spake of been
Mere gold — but this was all of that true steel   65
Whereof they forged the brand Excalibur, *arthurs sword,*
And lightnings play'd about it in the storm,
And all the little fowl were flurried at it,
And there were cries and clashings in the nest,
That sent him from his senses: let me go."   70

Then Bellicent bemoan'd herself and said,
" Hast thou no pity upon my loneliness?
Lo, where thy father Lot beside the hearth
Lies like a log, and all but smoulder'd out!
For ever since when traitor to the King   75
He fought against him in the barons' war,
And Arthur gave him back his territory,
His age hath slowly droopt, and now lies there
A yet-warm corpse, and yet unburiable,
No more; nor sees, nor hears, nor speaks, nor knows, 80
And both thy brethren are in Arthur's hall,
Albeit neither loved with that full love
I feel for thee, nor worthy such a love.
Stay therefore thou; red berries charm the bird,
And thee, mine innocent, the jousts, the wars,   85
Who never knewest finger-ache, nor pang
Of wrench'd or broken limb — an often chance
In those brain-stunning shocks, and tourney-falls,
Frights to my heart; but stay: follow the deer
By these tall firs and our fast-falling burns;   90
So make thy manhood mightier day by day;
Sweet is the chase: and I will seek thee out
Some comfortable bride and fair, to grace

Thy climbing life, and cherish my prone year,
Till falling into Lot's forgetfulness   95
I know not thee, myself, nor anything.
Stay, my best son! ye are yet more boy than man."

Then Gareth : "An ye hold me yet for child,
Hear yet once more the story of the child.
For, mother, there was once a king, like ours.   100
The prince his heir, when tall and marriageable,
Ask'd for a bride ; and thereupon the king
Set two before him. One was fair, strong, arm'd —
But to be won by force — and many men
Desired her ; one, good lack, no man desired.   105
And these were the conditions of the king :
That save he won the first by force, he needs
Must wed that other, whom no man desired,
A red-faced bride who knew herself so vile
That evermore she long'd to hide herself,   110
Nor fronted man or woman, eye to eye —
Yea — some she cleaved to, but they died of her.
And one — they call'd her Fame ; and one — O
        mother,
How can ye keep me tether'd to you ? — Shame.
Man am I grown, a man's work must I do.   115
Follow the deer ? follow the Christ, the King,
Live pure, speak true, right wrong, follow the King —
Else, wherefore born ? "

                    To whom the mother said :
" Sweet son, for there be many who deem him not,
Or will not deem him, wholly proven King —   120
Albeit in mine own heart I knew him King
When I was frequent with him in my youth,
And heard him kingly speak, and doubted him

No more than he, himself ; but felt him mine,
Of closest kin to me : yet — wilt thou leave   125
Thine easeful biding here, and risk thine all,
Life, limbs, for one that is not proven King?
Stay, till the cloud that settles round his birth
Hath lifted but a little. Stay, sweet son.''

And Gareth answer'd quickly : '' Not an hour,   130
So that ye yield me — I will walk thro' fire,
Mother, to gain it — your full leave to go.
Not proven, who swept the dust of ruin'd Rome
From off the threshold of the realm, and crush'd
The idolaters, and made the people free ?   135
Who should be king save him who makes us free ? ''

So when the Queen, who long had sought in vain
To break him from the intent to which he grew,
Found her son's will unwaveringly one,
She answer'd craftily : '' Will ye walk thro' fire ?   140
Who walks thro' fire will hardly heed the smoke.
Ay, go then, an ye must : only one proof,
Before thou ask the King to make thee knight,
Of thine obedience and thy love to me,
Thy mother, — I demand.''

And Gareth cried :   145
'' A hard one, or a hundred, so I go.
Nay — quick ! the proof to prove me to the quick ! ''

But slowly spake the mother looking at him :
'' Prince, thou shalt go disguised to Arthur's hall,
And hire thyself to serve for meats and drinks   150
Among the scullions and the kitchen-knaves,
And those that hand the dish across the bar.

Nor shalt thou tell thy name to any one.
And thou shalt serve a twelvemonth and a day."

    For so the Queen believed that when her son   155
Beheld his only way to glory lead
Low down thro' villain kitchen-vassalage,
Her own true Gareth was too princely-proud
To pass thereby ; so should he rest with her,
Closed in her castle from the sound of arms.   160

    Silent awhile was Gareth, then replied :
" The thrall in person may be free in soul,
And I shall see the jousts. Thy son am I,
And, since thou art my mother, must obey.
I therefore yield me freely to thy will ;   165
For hence will I, disguised, and hire myself
To serve with scullions and with kitchen-knaves ;
Nor tell my name to any — no, not the King."

    Gareth awhile linger'd. The mother's eye
Full of the wistful fear that he would go,   170
And turning toward him wheresoe'er he turn'd,
Perplext his outward purpose, till an hour
When, waken'd by the wind which with full voice
Swept bellowing thro' the darkness on to dawn,
He rose, and out of slumber calling two   175
That still had tended on him from his birth,
Before the wakeful mother heard him, went.

    The three were clad like tillers of the soil.
Southward they set their faces. The birds made
Melody on branch and melody in mid air.   180
The damp hill-slopes were quicken'd into green,
And the live green had kindled into flowers,
For it was past the time of Easter-day.

So, when their feet were planted on the plain
That broaden'd toward the base of Camelot,   185
Far off they saw the silver-misty morn
Rolling her smoke about the royal mount,
That rose between the forest and the field.
At times the summit of the high city flash'd;
At times the spires and turrets half-way down   190
Prick'd thro' the mist; at times the great gate shone
Only, that open'd on the field below:
Anon, the whole fair city had disappear'd.

Then those who went with Gareth were amazed,
One crying, "Let us go no further, lord: 195
Here is a city of enchanters, built
By fairy kings." The second echo'd him,
"Lord, we have heard from our wise man at home
To northward, that this king is not the King,
But only changeling out of Fairyland,   200
Who drave the heathen hence by sorcery
And Merlin's glamour." Then the first again,
"Lord, there is no such city anywhere,
But all a vision."

                Gareth answer'd them
With laughter, swearing he had glamour enow   205
In his own blood, his princedom, youth, and hopes,
To plunge old Merlin in the Arabian sea;
So push'd them all unwilling toward the gate.
And there was no gate like it under heaven.
For barefoot on the keystone, which was lined   210
And rippled like an ever-fleeting wave,
The Lady of the Lake stood: all her dress
Wept from her sides as water flowing away;
But like the cross her great and goodly arms

Stretch'd under all the cornice and upheld :   215
And drops of water fell from either hand;
And down from one a sword was hung, from one
A censer, either worn with wind and storm;
And o'er her breast floated the sacred fish;
And in the space to left of her, and right,   220
Were Arthur's wars in weird devices done,
New things and old co-twisted, as if Time
Were nothing, so inveterately that men
Were giddy gazing there; and over all
High on the top were those three queens, the friends 225
Of Arthur, who should help him at his need.

Then those with Gareth for so long a space
Stared at the figures that at last it seem'd
The dragon-boughts and elvish emblemings
Began to move, seethe, twine, and curl : they call'd 230
To Gareth, "Lord, the gateway is alive."

And Gareth likewise on them fixt his eyes
So long that even to him they seem'd to move.
Out of the city a blast of music peal'd.
Back from the gate started the three, to whom   235
From out thereunder came an ancient man,
Long-bearded, saying, "Who be ye, my sons?"

Then Gareth : "We be tillers of the soil,
Who leaving share in furrow come to see
The glories of our King: but these, my men, —   240
Your city moved so weirdly in the mist —
Doubt if the King be king at all, or come
From Fairyland ; and whether this be built
By magic, and by fairy kings and queens ;
Or whether there be any city at all,   245

Or all a vision : and this music now
Hath scared them both, but tell thou these the truth."

Then that old Seer made answer, playing on him
And saying: "Son, I have seen the good ship sail
Keel upward, and mast downward, in the heavens. 250
And solid turrets topsy-turvy in the air :
And here is truth ; but an it please thee not,
Take thou the truth as thou hast told it me.
For truly, as thou sayest, a fairy king
And fairy queens have built the city, son ;   255
They came from out a sacred mountain cleft
Toward the sunrise, each with harp in hand,
And built it to the music of their harps.
And, as thou sayest, it is enchanted, son,
For there is nothing in it as it seems   260
Saving the King; tho' some there be that hold
The King a shadow, and the city real :
Yet take thou heed of him, for, so thou pass
Beneath this archway, then wilt thou become
A thrall to his enchantments, for the King   265
Will bind thee by such vows as is a shame
A man should not be bound by, yet the which
No man can keep; but, so thou dread to swear
Pass not beneath this gateway, but abide
Without, among the cattle of the field.   270
For an ye heard a music, like enow
They are building still, seeing the city is built
To music, therefore never built at all,
And therefore built for ever."

Gareth spake
Anger'd : "Old master, reverence thine own beard 275
That looks as white as utter truth, and seems

Wellnigh as long as thou art statured tall!
Why mockest thou the stranger that hath been
To thee fair-spoken?"

                But the Seer replied:
" Know ye not then the Riddling of the Bards: 280
' Confusion, and illusion, and relation,
Elusion, and occasion, and evasion?'
I mock thee not but as thou mockest me,
And all that see thee, for thou art not who
Thou seemest, but I know thee who thou art.   285
And now thou goest up to mock the King,
Who cannot brook the shadow of any lie."

  Unmockingly the mocker ending here
Turn'd to the right, and past along the plain;
Whom Gareth looking after said; " My men,   290
Our one white lie sits like a little ghost
Here on the threshold of our enterprise.
Let love be blamed for it, not she, nor I:
Well, we will make amends."

               With all good cheer
He spake and laugh'd, then enter'd with his twain 295
Camelot, a city of shadowy palaces
And stately, rich in emblem and the work
Of ancient kings who did their days in stone;
Which Merlin's hand, the Mage at Arthur's court,
Knowing all arts, had touch'd, and everywhere,   300
At Arthur's ordinance, tipt with lessening peak
And pinnacle, and had made it spire to heaven.
And ever and anon a knight would pass
Outward, or inward to the hall: his arms
Clash'd; and the sound was good to Gareth's ear. 305

And out of bower and casement shyly glanced
Eyes of pure women, wholesome stars of love;
And all about a healthful people stept
As in the presence of a gracious king.

Then into hall Gareth ascending heard   310
A voice, the voice of Arthur, and beheld
Far over heads in that long-vaulted hall
The splendor of the presence of the King
Throned, and delivering doom — and looked no
    more —
But felt his young heart hammering in his ears   315
And thought, "For this half shadow of a lie
The truthful King will doom me when I speak."
Yet pressing on, tho' all in fear to find
Sir Gawain or Sir Modred, saw nor one
Nor other, but in all the listening eyes   320
Of those tall knights that ranged about the throne
Clear honor shining like the dewy star
Of dawn, and faith in their great King, with pure
Affection, and the light of victory,
And glory gain'd, and evermore to gain.   325

Then came a widow crying to the King:
"A boon, Sir King? Thy father, Uther, reft
From my dead lord a field with violence;
For howsoe'er at first he proffer'd gold,
Yet, for the field was pleasant in our eyes,   330
We yielded not, and then he reft us of it
Perforce and left us neither gold nor field."

Said Arthur, "Whether would ye? gold or field?"
To whom the woman weeping, "Nay, my lord,
The field was pleasant in my husband's eye."   335

And Arthur: "Have thy pleasant field again,
And thrice the gold for Uther's use thereof,
According to the years. No boon is here,
But justice, so thy say be proven true.
Accursed, who from the wrongs his father did   340
Would shape himself a right!"

              And while she past,
Came yet another widow crying to him:
"A boon, Sir King! Thine enemy, King, am I.
With thine own hand thou slewest my dear lord,
A knight of Uther in the barons' war,   345
When Lot and many another rose and fought
Against thee, saying thou wert basely born.
I held with these, and loathe to ask thee aught.
Yet lo! my husband's brother had my son
Thrall'd in his castle, and hath starved him dead, 350
And standeth seized of that inheritance
Which thou that slewest the sire hast left the son.
So, tho' I scarce can ask it thee for hate,
Grant me some knight to do the battle for me,
Kill the foul thief, and wreak me for my son."   355

Then strode a good knight forward, crying to him,
"A boon, Sir King! I am her kinsman, I.
Give me to right her wrong, and slay the man."

Then came Sir Kay; the seneschal, and cried,
"A boon, Sir King! even that thou grant her none, 360
This railer, that hath mock'd thee in full hall —
None; or the wholesome boon of gyve and gag."

But Arthur: "We sit King, to help the wrong'd
Thro' all our realm. The woman loves her lord.

Peace to thee, woman, with thy loves and hates !   365
The kings of old had doom'd thee to the flames ;
Aurelius Emrys would have scourged thee dead,
And Uther slit thy tongue : but get thee hence —
Lest that rough humor of the kings of old
Return upon me ! Thou that art her kin,   370
Go likewise ; lay him low and slay him not,
But bring him here, that I may judge the right,
According to the justice of the King :
Then, be he guilty, by that deathless King
Who lived and died for men, the man shall die." 375

Then came in hall the messenger of Mark,
A name of evil savor in the land,
The Cornish king. In either hand he bore
What dazzled all, and shone far-off as shines
A field of charlock in the sudden sun   380
Between two showers, a cloth of palest gold,
Which down he laid before the throne, and knelt,
Delivering that his lord, the vassal king,
Was ev'n upon his way to Camelot ;
For having heard that Arthur of his grace   385
Had made his goodly cousin Tristram knight,
And, for himself was of the greater state,
Being a king, he trusted his liege-lord
Would yield him this large honor all the more ;
So pray'd him well to accept this cloth of gold, 390
In token of true heart and fealty.

Then Arthur cried to rend the cloth, to rend
In pieces, and so cast it on the hearth.
An oak-tree smoulder'd there. "The goodly knight!
What! shall the shield of Mark stand among
        these?"   395

For, midway down the side of that long hall,
A stately pile, — whereof along the front,
Some blazon'd, some but carven, and some blank,
There ran a treble range of stony shields, —
Rose, and high-arching over-brow'd the hearth.   400
And under every shield a knight was named.
For this was Arthur's custom in his hall:
When some good knight had done one noble deed,
His arms were carven only; but if twain,
His arms were blazon'd also; but if none,   405
The shield was blank and bare, without a sign
Saving the name beneath: and Gareth saw
The shield of Gawain blazon'd rich and bright,
And Modred's blank as death; and Arthur cried
To rend the cloth and cast it on the hearth.   410

" More like are we to reave him of his crown
Than make him knight because men call him king.
The kings we found, ye know we stay'd their
          hands
From war among themselves, but left them kings;
Of whom were any bounteous, merciful,   415
Truth-speaking, brave, good livers, them we enroll'd
Among us, and they sit within our hall.
But Mark hath tarnish'd the great name of king,
As Mark would sully the low state of churl;
And, seeing he hath sent us cloth of gold,   420
Return, and meet, and hold him from our eyes,
Lest we should lap him up in cloth of lead,
Silenced for ever — craven — a man of plots,
Craft, poisonous counsels, wayside ambushings —
No fault of thine: let Kay the seneschal   425
Look to thy wants, and send thee satisfied —
Accursed, who strikes nor lets the hand be seen!"

And many another suppliant crying came
With noise of ravage wrought by beast and man,
And evermore a knight would ride away.   430

Last, Gareth leaning both hands heavily
Down on the shoulders of the twain, his men,
Approach'd between them toward the King, and ask'd,
"A boon, Sir King," — his voice was all ashamed, —
"For see ye not how weak and hunger-worn   435
I seem — leaning on these? grant me to serve
For meat and drink among thy kitchen-knaves
A twelvemonth and a day, nor seek my name.
Hereafter I will fight."

                              To him the King:
"A goodly youth and worth a goodlier boon!   440
But so thou wilt no goodlier, then must Kay,
The master of the meats and drinks, be thine."

He rose and past; then Kay, a man of mien
Wan-sallow as the plant that feels itself
Root-bitten by white lichen:

                              "Lo ye now!   445
This fellow hath broken from some abbey, where,
God wot, he had not beef and brewis enow,
However that might chance! but an he work,
Like any pigeon will I cram his crop,
And sleeker shall he shine than any hog."   450

Then Lancelot standing near: "Sir Seneschal,
Sleuth-hound thou knowest, and gray, and all the
                    hounds;
A horse thou knowest, a man thou dost not know:

Broad brows and fair, a fluent hair and fine,
High nose, a nostril large and fine, and hands   455
Large, fair, and fine ! — Some young lad's mystery —
But, or from sheepcot or king's hall, the boy
Is noble-natured. Treat him with all grace,
Lest he should come to shame thy judging of him."

Then Kay : " What murmurest thou of mystery ?   460
Think ye this fellow will poison the King's dish ?
Nay, for he spake too fool-like : mystery !
Tut, an the lad were noble, he had ask'd
For horse and armor : fair and fine, forsooth !
Sir Fine-face, Sir Fair-hands ? but see thou to it   465
That thine own fineness, Lancelot, some fine day
Undo thee not — and leave my man to me."

So Gareth all for glory underwent
The sooty yoke of kitchen-vassalage,
Ate with young lads his portion by the door,   470
And couch'd at night with grimy kitchen-knaves.
And Lancelot ever spake him pleasantly,
But Kay the seneschal, who loved him not,
Would hustle and harry him, and labor him
Beyond his comrade of the hearth, and set   475
To turn the broach, draw water, or hew wood,
Or grosser tasks ; and Gareth bow'd himself
With all obedience to the King, and wrought
All kind of service with a noble ease
That graced the lowliest act in doing it.   480
And when the thralls had talk among themselves,
And one would praise the love that linkt the King
And Lancelot — how the King had saved his life
In battle twice, and Lancelot once the King's —
For Lancelot was first in the tournament,   485

But Arthur mightiest on the battlefield —
Gareth was glad. Or if some other told
How once the wandering forester at dawn,
Far over the blue tarns and hazy seas,
On Caer-Eryri's highest found the King,   490
A naked babe, of whom the Prophet spake,
" He passes to the Isle Avilion,
He passes and is heal'd and cannot die " —
Gareth was glad. But if their talk were foul,
Then would he whistle rapid as any lark,   495
Or carol some old roundelay, and so loud
That first they mock'd but, after, reverenced him.
Or Gareth, telling some prodigious tale
Of knights who sliced a red life-bubbling way
Thro' twenty folds of twisted dragon, held   500
All in a gap-mouth'd circle his good mates
Lying or sitting round him, idle hands,
Charm'd ; till Sir Kay, the seneschal, would come
Blustering upon them, like a sudden wind
Among dead leaves, and drive them all apart.   505
Or when the thralls had sport among themselves,
So there were any trial of mastery,
He, by two yards in casting bar or stone,
Was counted best ; and if there chanced a joust,
So that Sir Kay nodded him leave to go,   510
Would hurry thither, and when he saw the knights
Clash like the coming and retiring wave,
And the spear spring, and good horse reel, the boy
Was half beyond himself for ecstasy.

So for a month he wrought among the thralls ; 515
But in the weeks that follow'd, the good Queen,
Repentant of the word she made him swear,
And saddening in her childless castle, sent,

Between the in-crescent and de-crescent moon,
Arms for her son, and loosed him from his vow.   520

  This, Gareth hearing from a squire of Lot
With whom he used to play at tourney once,
When both were children, and in lonely haunts
Would scratch a ragged oval on the sand,
And each at either dash from either end —   525
Shame never made girl redder than Gareth joy.
He laugh'd; he sprang. "Out of the smoke, at once
I leap from Satan's foot to Peter's knee —
These news be mine, none other's — nay, the King's —
Descend into the city:" whereon he sought   530
The King alone, and found, and told him all.

  "I have stagger'd thy strong Gawain in a tilt
For pastime; yea, he said it: joust can I.
Make me thy knight — in secret! let my name
Be hidd'n, and give me the first quest, I spring   535
Like flame from ashes."

                    Here the King's calm eye
Fell on, and check'd, and made him flush, and bow
Lowly, to kiss his hand, who answer'd him:
"Son, the good mother let me know thee here,
And sent her wish that I would yield thee thine.   540
Make thee my knight? my knights are sworn to
    vows
Of utter hardihood, utter gentleness,
And, loving, utter faithfulness in love,
And uttermost obedience to the King."

  Then Gareth, lightly springing from his knees: 545
"My King, for hardihood I can promise thee.

For uttermost obedience make demand
Of whom ye gave me to, the Seneschal,
No mellow master of the meats and drinks!
And as for love, God wot, I love not yet,   550
But love I shall, God willing."

                       And the King:
" Make thee my knight in secret? yea, but he,
Our noblest brother, and our truest man,
And one with me in all, he needs must know."

      " Let Lancelot know, my King, let Lancelot
          know.   555
Thy noblest and thy truest!"

                       And the King:
" But wherefore would ye men should wonder at you?
Nay, rather for the sake of me, their King,
And the deed's sake my knighthood do the deed,
Than to be noised of."

                  Merrily Gareth ask'd: 560
"Have I not earn'd my cake in baking of it?
Let be my name until I make my name!
My deeds will speak: it is but for a day."
So with a kindly hand on Gareth's arm
Smiled the great King, and half-unwillingly   565
Loving his lusty youthhood yielded to him.
Then, after summoning Lancelot privily:
" I have given him the first quest: he is not proven.
Look therefore, when he calls for this in hall,
Thou get to horse and follow him far away.   570
Cover the lions on thy shield, and see,
Far as thou mayest, he be nor ta'en nor slain."

Then that same day there past into the hall
A damsel of high lineage, and a brow
May-blossom, and a cheek of apple-blossom,   575
Hawk-eyes; and lightly was her slender nose
Tip-tilted like the petal of a flower:
She into hall past with her page and cried:

"O King, for thou hast driven the foe without,
See to the foe within! bridge, ford, beset   580
By bandits, every one that owns a tower
The lord for half a league. Why sit ye there?
Rest would I not, Sir King, an I were king,
Till even the lonest hold were all as free
From cursed bloodshed as thine altar-cloth   585
From that best blood it is a sin to spill."

"Comfort thyself," said Arthur, "I nor mine
Rest: so my knighthood keep the vows they swore,
The wastest moorland of our realm shall be
Safe, damsel, as the centre of this hall.   590
What is thy name? thy need?"

                              "My name?" she said —
"Lynette, my name; noble; my need, a knight
To combat for my sister, Lyonors,
A lady of high lineage, of great lands,
And comely, yea, and comelier than myself.   595
She lives in Castle Perilous: a river
Runs in three loops about her living-place;
And o'er it are three passings, and three knights
Defend the passings, brethren, and a fourth,
And of that four the mightiest, holds her stay'd   600
In her own castle, and so besieges her
To break her will, and make her wed with him;

And but delays his purport till thou send
To do the battle with him thy chief man
Sir Lancelot, whom he trusts to overthrow;   605
Then wed, with glory : but she will not wed
Save whom she loveth, or a holy life.
Now therefore have I come for Lancelot."

Then Arthur mindful of Sir Gareth ask'd :
"Damsel, ye know this Order lives to crush   610
All wrongers of the realm. But say, these four,
Who be they? What the fashion of the men?"

"They be of foolish fashion, O Sir King,
The fashion of that old knight-errantry
Who ride abroad, and do but what they will;   615
Courteous or bestial from the moment, such
As have nor law nor king ; and three of these
Proud in their fantasy call themselves the Day,
Morning-Star, and Noon-Sun, and Evening-Star,
Being strong fools ; and never a whit more wise   620
The fourth, who alway rideth arm'd in black,
A huge man-beast of boundless savagery.
He names himself the Night and oftener Death,
And wears a helmet mounted with a skull,
And bears a skeleton figured on his arms,   625
To show that who may slay or scape the three,
Slain by himself, shall enter endless night.
And all these four be fools, but mighty men,
And therefore am I come for Lancelot."

Hereat Sir Gareth call'd from where he rose,   630
A head with kindling eyes above the throng,
"A boon, Sir King — this quest!" then — for he
     mark'd

Kay near him groaning like a wounded bull —
" Yea, King, thou knowest thy kitchen-knave am I,
And mighty thro' thy meats and drinks am I,   635
And I can topple over a hundred such.
Thy promise, King," and Arthur glancing at him,
Brought down a momentary brow. " Rough, sudden,
And pardonable, worthy to be knight —
Go therefore," and all hearers were amazed.   640

But on the damsel's forehead shame, pride, wrath
Slew the may-white : she lifted either arm,
" Fie on thee, King ! I ask'd for thy chief knight,
And thou hast given me but a kitchen-knave."
Then ere a man in hall could stay her, turn'd,   645
Fled down the lane of access to the King,
Took horse, descended the slope street, and past
The weird white gate, and paused without, beside
The field of tourney, murmuring " kitchen-knave ! "

Now two great entries open'd from the hall,   650
At one end that gave upon a range
Of level pavement where the King would pace
At sunrise, gazing over plain and wood ;
And down from this a lordly stairway sloped
Till lost in blowing trees and tops of towers ;   655
And out by this main doorway past the King.
But one was counter to the hearth, and rose
High that the highest-crested helm could ride
Therethro' nor graze ; and by this entry fled
The damsel in her wrath, and on to this   660
Sir Gareth strode, and saw without the door
King Arthur's gift, the worth of half a town,
A war-horse of the best, and near it stood
The two that out of north had follow'd him.

This bare a maiden shield, a casque; that held   665
The horse, the spear; whereat Sir Gareth loosed
A cloak that dropt from collar-bone to heel,
A cloth of roughest web, and cast it down,
And from it, like a fuel-smother'd fire
That lookt half-dead, brake bright, and flash'd as
      those   670
Dull-coated things, that making slide apart
Their dusk wing-cases, all beneath there burns
A jewell'd harness, ere they pass and fly.
So Gareth ere he parted flash'd in arms.
Then as he donn'd the helm, and took the shield   675
And mounted horse and graspt a spear, of grain
Storm-strengthen'd on a windy site, and tipt
With trenchant steel, around him slowly prest
The people, while from out of kitchen came
The thralls in throng, and seeing who had work'd   680
Lustier than any, and whom they could but love,
Mounted in arms, threw up their caps and cried,
"God bless the King, and all his fellowship!"
And on thro' lanes of shouting Gareth rode
Down the slope street, and past without the gate.   685

   So Gareth past with joy; but as the cur
Pluckt from the cur he fights with, ere his cause
Be cool'd by fighting, follows, being named,
His owner, but remembers all, and growls
Remembering, so Sir Kay beside the door   690
Mutter'd in scorn of Gareth whom he used
To harry and hustle.

                    "Bound upon a quest
With horse and arms — the King hath past his time —
My scullion knave! Thralls, to your work again,

For an your fire be low ye kindle mine!　695
Will there be dawn in West and eve in East?
Begone! — my knave! — belike and like enow
Some old head-blow not heeded in his youth
So shook his wits they wander in his prime —
Crazed! How the villain lifted up his voice,　700
Nor shamed to bawl himself a kitchen-knave!
Tut, he was tame and meek enow with me,
Till peacock'd up with Lancelot's noticing.
Well — I will after my loud knave, and learn
Whether he know me for his master yet.　705
Out of the smoke he came, and so my lance
Hold, by God's grace, he shall into the mire —
Thence, if the King awaken from his craze,
Into the smoke again."

　　　　　　　　But Lancelot said:
"Kay, wherefore wilt thou go against the King,　710
For that did never he whereon ye rail,
But ever meekly served the King in thee?
Abide: take counsel; for this lad is great
And lusty, and knowing both of lance and sword."
"Tut, tell not me," said Kay, "ye are overfine　715
To mar stout knaves with foolish courtesies":
Then mounted, on thro' silent faces rode
Down the slope city, and out beyond the gate.

　　But by the field of tourney lingering yet
Mutter'd the damsel: "Wherefore did the King　720
Scorn me? for, were Sir Lancelot lackt, at least
He might have yielded to me one of those
Who tilt for lady's love and glory here,
Rather than — O sweet heaven! O fie upon him! —
His kitchen-knave."

To whom Sir Gareth drew — 725
And there were none but few goodlier than he —
Shining in arms, " Damsel, the quest is mine.
Lead, and I follow." She thereat, as one
That smells a foul-flesh'd agaric in the holt,
And deems it carrion of some woodland thing,   730
Or shrew, or weasel, nipt her slender nose
With petulant thumb and finger, shrilling, " Hence!
Avoid, thou smellest all of kitchen-grease.
And look who comes behind"; for there was Kay.
" Knowest thou not me? thy master? I am Kay.   735
We lack thee by the hearth."

And Gareth to him,
" Master no more! too well I know thee, ay —
The most ungentle knight in Arthur's hall."
" Have at thee then," said Kay: they shock'd, and
          Kay
Fell shoulder-slipt, and Gareth cried again,   740
" Lead, and I follow," and fast away she fled.

But after sod and shingle ceased to fly
Behind her, and the heart of her good horse
Was nigh to burst with violence of the beat,
Perforce she stay'd, and overtaken spoke: 745

" What doest thou, scullion, in my fellowship?
Deem'st thou that I accept thee aught the more
Or love thee better, that by some device
Full cowardly, or by mere unhappiness,
Thou hast overthrown and slain thy master —
          thou! —   750
Dish-washer and broach-turner, loon! — to me
Thou smellest all of kitchen as before."

"Damsel," Sir Gareth answer'd gently, "say
Whate'er ye will, but whatso'er ye say,
I leave not till I finish this fair quest,   755
Or die therefore."

                "Ay, wilt thou finish it?
Sweet lord, how like a noble knight he talks!
The listening rogue hath caught the manner of it.
But, knave, anon thou shalt be met with, knave,
And then by such a one that thou for all   760
The kitchen brewis that was ever supt
Shalt not once dare to look him in the face."

"I shall assay," said Gareth with a smile
That madden'd her, and away she flashed again
Down the long avenues of a boundless wood,   765
And Gareth following was again beknaved:

"Sir Kitchen-knave, I have miss'd the only way
Where Arthur's men are set along the wood;
The wood is nigh as full of thieves as leaves:
If both be slain, I am rid of thee; but yet,   770
Sir Scullion, canst thou use that spit of thine?
Fight, an thou canst: I have miss'd the only way."

So till the dusk that follow'd evensong
Rode on the two, reviler and reviled;
Then after one long slope was mounted, saw,   775
Bowl-shaped, thro' tops of many thousand pines
A gloomy-gladed hollow slowly sink
To westward — in the deeps whereof a mere,
Round as the red eye of an eagle-owl,
Under the half-dead sunset glared; and shouts   780
Ascended, and there brake a servingman

Flying from out of the black wood, and crying,
"They have bound my lord to cast him in the
      mere."
Then Gareth, "Bound am I to right the wrong'd,
But straitlier bound am I to bide with thee."   785
And when the damsel spake contemptuously,
"Lead, and I follow," Gareth cried again,
"Follow, I lead!" so down among the pines
He plunged; and there, black-shadow'd nigh the mere,
And mid-thigh-deep in bulrushes and reed,   790
Saw six tall men haling a seventh along,
A stone about his neck to drown him in it.
Three with good blows he quieted, but three
Fled thro' the pines; and Gareth loosed the stone
From off his neck, then in the mere beside   795
Tumbled it; oilily bubbled up the mere.
Last, Gareth loosed his bonds and on free feet
Set him, a stalwart baron, Arthur's friend.

"Well that ye came, or else these caitiff rogues
Had wreak'd themselves on me; good cause is theirs 800
To hate me, for my wont hath ever been
To catch my thief, and then like vermin here
Drown him, and with a stone about his neck;
And under this wan water many of them
Lie rotting, but at night let go the stone,   805
And rise, and flickering in a grimly light
Dance on the mere. Good now, ye have saved a life
Worth somewhat as the cleanser of this wood.
And fain would I reward thee worshipfully.
What guerdon will ye?"

           Gareth sharply spake: 810
"None! for the deed's sake have I done the deed,

In uttermost obedience to the King.
But wilt thou yield this damsel harborage?"

Whereat the baron saying, "I well believe
You be of Arthur's Table," a light laugh   815
Broke from Lynette: "Ay, truly of a truth,
And in a sort, being Arthur's kitchen-knave!—
But deem not I accept thee aught the more,
Scullion, for running sharply with thy spit
Down on a rout of craven foresters.   820
A thresher with his flail had scatter'd them.
Nay — for thou smellest of the kitchen still.
But an this lord will yield us harborage,
Well."

   So she spake. A league beyond the wood
All in a full-fair manor and a rich,   825
His towers, where that day a feast had been
Held in high hall, and many a viand left,
And many a costly cate, received the three.
And there they placed a peacock in his pride
Before the damsel, and the baron set   830
Gareth beside her, but at once she rose.

"Meseems, that here is much discourtesy,
Setting this knave, Lord Baron, at my side.
Hear me — this morn I stood in Arthur's hall,
And pray'd the King would grant me Lancelot   835
To fight the brotherhood of Day and Night—
The last a monster unsubduable
Of any save of him for whom I call'd —
Suddenly bawls this frontless kitchen-knave,
'The quest is mine; thy kitchen-knave am I,   840
And mighty thro' thy meats and drinks am I.'

•

Then Arthur all at once gone mad replies,
'Go therefore,' and so gives the quest to him—
Him—here—a villain fitter to stick swine
Than ride abroad redressing women's wrong,   845
Or sit beside a noble gentlewoman."

Then half-ashamed and part-amazed, the lord
Now look'd at one and now at other, left
The damsel by the peacock in his pride,
And, seating Gareth at another board,   850
Sat down beside him, ate and then began:

"Friend, whether thou be kitchen-knave, or not,
Or whether it be the maiden's fantasy,
And whether she be mad, or else the King,
Or both or neither, or thyself be mad,   855
I ask not: but thou strikest a strong stroke,
For strong thou art and goodly therewithal,
And saver of my life; and therefore now,
For here be mighty men to joust with, weigh
Whether thou wilt not with thy damsel back   860
To crave again Sir Lancelot of the King.
Thy pardon; I but speak for thine avail,
The saver of my life."

                            And Gareth said,
"Full pardon, but I follow up the quest,
Despite of Day and Night and Death and Hell."   865

So when, next morn, the lord whose life he saved
Had, some brief space, convey'd them on their way
And left them with God-speed, Sir Gareth spake,
"Lead, and I follow." Haughtily she replied:

"I fly no more: I allow thee for an hour.   870
Lion and stoat have isled together, knave,
In time of flood. Nay, furthermore, methinks
Some ruth is mine for thee. Back wilt thou, fool?
For hard by here is one will overthrow
And slay thee; then will I to court again,   875
And shame the King for only yielding me
My champion from the ashes of his hearth."

To whom Sir Gareth answer'd courteously:
"Say thou thy say, and I will do my deed.
Allow me for mine hour, and thou wilt find   880
My fortunes all as fair as hers who lay
Among the ashes and wedded the King's son."

Then to the shore of one of those long loops
Wherethro' the serpent river coil'd, they came.
Rough-thicketed were the banks and steep; the stream
Full, narrow; this a bridge of single arc   886
Took at a leap; and on the further side
Arose a silk pavilion, gay with gold
In streaks and rays, and all Lent-lily in hue,
Save that the dome was purple, and above,   890
Crimson, a slender banneret fluttering.
And therebefore the lawless warrior paced
Unarm'd, and calling, " Damsel, is this he,
The champion thou hast brought from Arthur's hall?
For whom we let thee pass." " Nay, nay," she said, 895
" Sir Morning-Star. The King in utter scorn
Of thee and thy much folly hath sent thee here
His kitchen-knave: and look thou to thyself:
See that he fall not on thee suddenly,
And slay thee unarm'd; he is not knight but
          knave."   900

Then at his call, "O daughters of the Dawn,
And servants of the Morning-Star, approach,
Arm me," from out the silken curtain-folds
Bare-footed and bare-headed three fair girls
In gilt and rosy raiment came: their feet   905
In dewy grasses glisten'd; and the hair
All over glanced with dewdrop or with gem
Like sparkles in the stone Avanturine.
These arm'd him in blue arms, and gave a shield
Blue also, and thereon the morning star.   910
And Gareth silent gazed upon the knight,
Who stood a moment, ere his horse was brought,
Glorying; and in the stream beneath him shone,
Immingled with heaven's azure waveringly,
The gay pavilion and the naked feet,   915
His arms, the rosy raiment, and the star.

Then she that watched him : "Wherefore stare ye so?
Thou shakest in thy fear: there yet is time:
Flee down the valley before he get to horse.
Who will cry shame? Thou art not knight but knave."

Said Gareth: "Damsel, whether knave or knight,   921
Far liefer had I fight a score of times
Than hear thee so missay me and revile.
Fair words were best for him who fights for thee;
But truly foul are better, for they send   925
That strength of anger thro' mine arms, I know
That I shall overthrow him."

                            And he that bore
The star, when mounted, cried from o'er the bridge:
"A kitchen-knave, and sent in scorn of me!
Such fight not I, but answer scorn with scorn.   930

For this were shame to do him further wrong.
Than set him on his feet, and take his horse
And arms, and so return him to the King.
Come, therefore, leave thy lady lightly, knave.
Avoid: for it beseemeth not a knave   935
To ride with such a lady."

        " Dog, thou liest!
I spring from loftier lineage than thine own."
He spake; and all at fiery speed the two
Shock'd on the central bridge, and either spear
Bent but not brake, and either knight at once,   940
Hurl'd as a stone from out of a catapult
Beyond his horse's crupper and the bridge,
Fell, as if dead; but quickly rose and drew,
And Gareth lash'd so fiercely with his brand
He drave his enemy backward down the bridge,   945
The damsel crying, " Well-stricken, kitchen-knave!"
Till Gareth's shield was cloven; but one stroke
Laid him that clove it grovelling on the ground.

 Then cried the fallen, " Take not my life: I yield."
And Gareth, " So this damsel ask it of me,   950
Good — I accord it easily as a grace."
She reddening, " Insolent scullion! I of thee?
I bound to thee for any favor ask'd!"
" Then shall he die." And Gareth there unlaced
His helmet as to slay him, but she shriek'd,   955
" Be not so hardy, scullion, as to slay
One nobler than thyself." " Damsel, thy charge
Is an abounding pleasure to me. Knight,
Thy life is thine at her command. Arise
And quickly pass to Arthur's hall, and say   960
His kitchen-knave hath sent thee. See thou crave

His pardon for thy breaking of his laws.
Myself when I return will plead for thee.
Thy shield is mine — farewell; and, damsel, thou,
Lead, and I follow."

        And fast away she fled; 965
Then when he came upon her, spake : " Methought,
Knave, when I watch'd thee striking on the bridge,
The savor of thy kitchen came upon me
A little faintlier: but the wind hath changed;
I scent it twenty-fold." And then she sang, 970

  " 'O morning star ' — not that tall felon there
Whom thou, by sorcery or unhappiness
Or some device, hast foully overthrown, —
' O morning star that smilest in the blue,
O star, my morning dream hath proven true, 975
Smile sweetly, thou! my love hath smiled on me.'

  " But thou begone, take counsel, and away,
For hard by here is one that guards a ford —
The second brother in their fool's parable —
Will pay thee all thy wages, and to boot. 980
Care not for shame: thou art not knight but knave."

  To whom Sir Gareth answer'd, laughingly :
" Parables ? Hear a parable of the knave.
When I was kitchen-knave among the rest,
Fierce was the hearth, and one of my co-mates 985
Own'd a rough dog, to whom he cast his coat,
'Guard it,' and there was none to meddle with it.
And such a coat art thou, and thee the King
Gave me to guard, and such a dog am I,
To worry, and not to flee — and — knight or knave — 990

The knave that doth thee service as full knight
Is all as good, meseems, as any knight
Toward thy sister's freeing."

                 " Ay, Sir Knave!
Ay, knave, because thou strikest as a knight,
Being but knave, I hate thee all the more."   995

    " Fair damsel, you should worship me the more,
That, being but knave, I throw thine enemies."

    " Ay, ay," she said " but thou shalt meet thy match."

    So when they touch'd the second river-loop,
Huge on a huge red horse, and all in mail   1000
Burnish'd to blinding, shone the Noonday Sun
Beyond a raging shallow. As if the flower
That blows a globe of after arrowlets
Ten-thousand-fold had grown, flash'd the fierce shield,
All sun ; and Gareth's eyes had flying blots   1005
Before them when he turn'd from watching him.
He from beyond the roaring shallow roar'd,
" What doest thou, brother, in my marches here ? "
And she athwart the shallow shrill'd again,
" Here is a kitchen-knave from Arthur's hall   1010
Hath overthrown thy brother, and hath his arms."
" Ugh ! " cried the Sun, and, vizoring up a red
And cipher face of rounded foolishness,
Push'd horse across the foamings of the ford,
Whom Gareth met mid-stream : no room was there 1015
For lance or tourney-skill : four strokes they struck
With sword, and these were mighty ; the new knight
Had fear he might be shamed ; but as the Sun
Heaved up a ponderous arm to strike the fifth,

The hoof of his horse slipt in the stream, the stream 1020
Descended, and the Sun was wash'd away.

Then Gareth laid his lance athwart the ford;
So drew him home; but he that fought no more,
As being all bone-batter'd on the rock,
Yielded; and Gareth sent him to the King.   1025
"Myself when I return will plead for thee.
Lead, and I follow." Quietly she led.
" Hath not the good wind, damsel, changed again?"
"Nay, not a point; nor art thou victor here.
There lies a ridge of slate across the ford;   1030
His horse thereon stumbled — ay, for I saw it.

"'O sun'—not this strong fool whom thou, Sir Knave,
Hast overthrown thro' mere unhappiness —
'O sun, that wakenest all to bliss or pain,
O moon, that layest all to sleep again,   1035
Shine sweetly: twice my love hath smiled on me.'

"What knowest thou of love-song or of love?
Nay, nay, God wot, so thou wert nobly born,
Thou hast a pleasant presence. Yea, perchance,—

"'O dewy flowers that open to the sun,   1040
O dewy flowers that close when day is done,
Blow sweetly: twice my love hath smiled on me.'

"What knowest thou of flowers, except, belike,
To garnish meats with? hath not our good King,
Who lent me thee, the flower of kitchendom,   1045
A foolish love for flowers? what stick ye round

The pasty? wherewithal deck the boar's head?
Flowers? nay, the boar hath rosemaries and bay.

" 'O birds that warble to the morning sky,
O birds that warble as the day goes by,   1050
Sing sweetly: twice my love hath smiled on me.'

" What knowest thou of birds, lark, mavis, merle,
Linnet? what dream ye when they utter forth
May-music growing with the growing light,
Their sweet sun-worship? these be for the snare — 1055
So runs thy fancy — these be for the spit,
Larding and basting. See thou have not now
Larded thy last, except thou turn and fly.
There stands the third fool of their allegory."

For there beyond a bridge of treble bow,   1060
All in a rose-red from the west, and all
Naked it seem'd, and glowing in the broad
Deep-dimpled current underneath, the knight
That named himself the Star of Evening stood.

And Gareth, " Wherefore waits the madman
        there   1065
Naked in open dayshine?" "Nay," she cried,
"Not naked, only wrapt in harden'd skins
That fit him like his own; and so ye cleave
His armor off him, these will turn the blade."

Then the third brother shouted o'er the bridge, 1070
" O brother-star, why shine ye here so low?
Thy ward is higher up: but have ye slain
The damsel's champion?" and the damsel cried:

"No star of thine, but shot from Arthur's heaven
With all disaster unto thine and thee!   1075
For both thy younger brethren have gone down
Before this youth; and so wilt thou, Sir Star;
Art thou not old?"

                    "Old, damsel, old and hard,
Old, with the might and breath of twenty boys."
Said Gareth, "Old, and over-bold in brag!   1080
But that same strength which threw the Morning Star
Can throw the Evening."

                    Then that other blew
A hard and deadly note upon the horn.
"Approach and arm me!" With slow steps from out
An old storm-beaten, russet, many-stain'd   1085
Pavilion, forth a grizzled damsel came,
And arm'd him in old arms, and brought a helm
With but a drying evergreen for crest,
And gave a shield whereon the star of even
Half-tarnish'd and half-bright, his emblem, shone. 1090
But when it glitter'd o'er the saddle-bow,
They madly hurl'd together on the bridge;
And Gareth overthrew him, lighted, drew,
There met him drawn, and overthrew him again,
But up like fire he started: and as oft   1095
As Gareth brought him grovelling on his knees,
So many a time he vaulted up again;
Till Gareth panted hard, and his great heart,
Foredooming all his trouble was in vain,
Labor'd within him, for he seem'd as one   1100
That all in later, sadder age begins
To war against ill uses of a life,
But these from all his life arise, and cry,

"Thou hast made us lords, and canst not put us
    down!"
He half despairs; so Gareth seem'd to strike   1105
Vainly, the damsel clamoring all the while,
"Well done, knave-knight, well stricken, O good
    knight-knave —
O knave, as noble as any of all the knights —
Shame me not, shame me not. I have prophesied —
Strike, thou art worthy of the Table Round —   1110
His arms are old, he trusts the harden'd skin —
Strike — strike — the wind will never change again."
And Gareth hearing ever stronglier smote,
And hew'd great pieces of his armor off him,
But lash'd in vain against the harden'd skin,   1115
And could not wholly bring him under, more
Than loud Southwesterns, rolling ridge on ridge,
The buoy that rides at sea, and dips and springs
For ever; till at length Sir Gareth's brand
Clash'd his, and brake it utterly to the hilt.   1120
"I have thee now"; but forth that other sprang,
And, all unknightlike, writhed his wiry arms
Around him, till he felt, despite his mail,
Strangled, but straining even his uttermost
Cast, and so hurl'd him headlong o'er the bridge 1125
Down to the river, sink or swim, and cried,
"Lead, and I follow."

                But the damsel said:
"I lead no longer; ride thou at my side;
Thou art the kingliest of all kitchen-knaves.

   "'O trefoil, sparkling on the rainy plain,   1130
O rainbow with three colors after rain,
Shine sweetly: thrice my love hath smiled on me.'

" Sir, — and good faith, I fain had added — Knight,
But that I heard thee call thyself a knave, —
Shamed am I that I so rebuked, reviled,   1135
Missaid thee; noble I am; and thought the King
Scorn'd me and mine; and now thy pardon, friend,
For thou hast ever answer'd courteously,
And wholly bold thou art, and meek withal
As any of Arthur's best, but, being knave,   1140
Hast mazed my wit: I marvel what thou art."

" Damsel," he said, " you be not all to blame,
Saving that you mistrusted our good King
Would handle scorn, or yield you, asking, one
Not fit to cope your quest. You said your say;   1145
Mine answer was my deed. Good sooth! I hold
He scarce is knight, yea but half-man, nor meet
To fight for gentle damsel, he, who lets
His heart be stirr'd with any foolish heat
At any gentle damsel's waywardness.   1150
Shamed? care not! thy foul sayings fought for
        me:
And seeing now thy words are fair, methinks
There rides no knight, not Lancelot, his great self,
Hath force to quell me."

                        Nigh upon that hour
When the lone hern forgets his melancholy,   1155
Lets down his other leg, and stretching dreams
Of goodly supper in the distant pool,
Then turn'd the noble damsel smiling at him,
And told him of a cavern hard at hand,
Where bread and baken meats and good red wine 1160
Of Southland, which the Lady Lyonors
Had sent her coming champion, waited him.

Anon they past a narrow comb wherein
Were slabs of rock with figures, knights on horse
Sculptured, and deckt in slowly-waning hues.   1165
" Sir Knave, my knight, a hermit, once was here,
Whose holy hand hath fashion'd on the rock
The war of Time against the soul of man.
And yon four fools have suck'd their allegory
From these damp walls, and taken but the form. 1170
Know ye not these?" and Gareth lookt and read —
In letters like to those the vexillary
Hath left crag-carven o'er the streaming Gelt —
" PHOSPHORUS," then " MERIDIES,"—" HESPERUS "—
" NOX "—" MORS," beneath five figures, armed men,
Slab after slab, their faces forward all,   1176
And running down the Soul, a shape that fled
With broken wings, torn raiment, and loose hair,
For help and shelter to the hermit's cave.
" Follow the faces, and we find it. Look,   1180
Who comes behind?"

                                        For one — delay'd at first
Thro' helping back the dislocated Kay
To Camelot, then by what thereafter chanced,
The damsel's headlong error thro' the wood —
Sir Lancelot, having swum the river-loops —   1185
His blue shield-lions cover'd — softly drew
Behind the twain, and when he saw the star
Gleam, on Sir Gareth's turning to him, cried,
" Stay, felon knight, I avenge me for my friend."
And Gareth crying prick'd against the cry;   1190
But when they closed — in a moment — at one touch
Of that skill'd spear, the wonder of the world —
Went sliding down so easily, and fell,
That when he found the grass within his hands

He laugh'd; the laughter jarr'd upon Lynette: 1195
Harshly she ask'd him, " Shamed and overthrown,
And tumbled back into the kitchen-knave,
Why laugh ye? that ye blew your boast in vain?"
" Nay, noble damsel, but that I, the son
Of old King Lot and good Queen Bellicent,   1200
And victor of the bridges and the ford,
And knight of Arthur, here lie thrown by whom
I know not, all thro' mere unhappiness —
Device and sorcery and unhappiness —
Out, sword; we are thrown!" And Lancelot
          answer'd: " Prince,   1205
O Gareth — thro' the mere unhappiness
Of one who came to help thee, not to harm,
Lancelot, and all as glad·to find thee whole
As on the day when Arthur knighted him."   1209

Then Gareth: " Thou — Lancelot! — thine the hand
That threw me? An some chance to mar the boast
Thy brethren of thee make — which could not chance —
Had sent thee down before a lesser spear,
Shamed had I been, and sad — O Lancelot — thou!"

Whereat the maiden, petulant: " Lancelot,   1215
Why came ye not when call'd? and wherefore now
Come ye, not call'd? I gloried in my knave,
Who being still rebuked would answer still
Courteous as any knight — but now, if knight,
The marvel dies, and leaves me fool'd and trick'd,   1220
And only wondering wherefore play'd upon;
And doubtful whether I and mine be scorn'd.
Where should be truth if not in Arthur's Hall,
In Arthur's presence? Knight, knave, prince and fool,
I hate thee and forever."

And Lancelot said: 1225
" Blessed be thou, Sir Gareth! knight art thou
To the King's best wish. O damsel, be you wise,
To call him shamed who is but overthrown?
Thrown have I been, nor once, but many a time.
Victor from vanquish'd issues at the last,   1230
And overthrower from being overthrown.
With sword we have not striven; and thy good horse
And thou art weary; yet not less I felt
Thy manhood thro' that wearied lance of thine.
Well hast thou done; for all the stream is freed,   1235
And thou hast wreak'd his justice on his foes,
And when reviled hast answer'd graciously,
And makest merry when overthrown. Prince, knight,
Hail, knight and prince, and of our Table Round!"

And then when turning to Lynette he told   1240
The tale of Gareth, petulantly she said:
" Ay, well — ay, well — for worse than being fool'd
Of others, is to fool one's self. A cave,
Sir Lancelot, is hard by, with meats and drinks
And forage for the horse, and flint for fire,   1245
But all about it flies a honeysuckle.
Seek, till we find." And when they sought and found,
Sir Gareth drank and ate, and all his life
Past into sleep: on whom the maiden gazed:
" Sound sleep be thine! sound cause to sleep hast thou.
Wake lusty! Seem I not as tender to him   1251
As any mother? Ay, but such a one
As all day long hath rated at her child,
And vext his day, but blesses him asleep —
Good lord, how sweetly smells the honeysuckle   1255
In the hush'd night, as if the world were one
Of utter peace, and love, and gentleness!

O Lancelot, Lancelot,"— and she clapt her hands —
" Full merry am I to find my goodly knave
Is knight and noble. See now, sworn have I,   1260
Else yon black felon had not let me pass,
To bring thee back to do the battle with him.
Thus an thou goest, he will fight thee first ;
Who doubts thee victor? so will my knight-knave
Miss the full flower of this accomplishment."   1265

Said Lancelot : " Peradventure he you name
May know my shield. Let Gareth, an he will,
Change his for mine and take my charger, fresh,
Not to be spurr'd, loving the battle as well
As he that rides him." " Lancelot-like," she said,   1270
" Courteous in this, Lord Lancelot, as in all."

And Gareth, wakening, fiercely clutch'd the shield :
" Ramp, ye lance-splintering lions, on whom all spears
Are rotten sticks ! ye seem agape to roar !
Yea, ramp and roar at leaving of your lord ! —   1275
Care not, good beasts, so well I care for you.
O noble Lancelot, from my hold on these
Streams virtue — fire — thro' one that will not shame
Even the shadow of Lancelot under shield.
Hence : let us go."

                          Silent the silent field   1280
They traversed. Arthur's Harp tho' summer-wan,
In counter motion to the clouds, allured
The glance of Gareth dreaming on his liege.
A star shot ; " Lo," said Gareth, " the foe falls !"
An owl whoopt : " Hark the victor pealing there !"   1285
Suddenly she that rode upon his left
Clung to the shield that Lancelot lent him, crying :

"Yield, yield him this again: 't is he must fight:
I curse the tongue that all thro' yesterday
Reviled thee, and hath wrought on Lancelot now 1290
To lend thee horse and shield: wonders ye have done;
Miracles ye cannot: here is glory enow
In having flung the three: I see thee maim'd,
Mangled; I swear thou canst not fling the fourth."

     "And wherefore, damsel? tell me all ye know. 1295
You cannot scare me; nor rough face, or voice,
Brute bulk of limb, or boundless savagery
Appal me from the quest."

                         "Nay, prince," she cried,
"God wot, I never look'd upon the face,
Seeing he never rides abroad by day;   1300
But watch'd him have I like a phantom pass
Chilling the night: nor have I heard the voice.
Always he made his mouthpiece of a page
Who came and went, and still reported him
As closing in himself the strength of ten,   1305
And when his anger tare him, massacring
Man, woman, lad, and girl — yea, the soft babe!
Some hold that he hath swallow'd infant flesh,
Monster! O prince, I went for Lancelot first,
The quest is Lancelot's: give him back the shield." 1310

     Said Gareth laughing, "An he fight for this,
Belike he wins it as the better man:
Thus — and not else!"

                         But Lancelot on him urged
All the devisings of their chivalry
When one might meet a mightier than himself; 1315

How best to manage horse, lance, sword, and shield,
And so fill up the gap where force might fail
With skill and fineness. Instant were his words.

  Then Gareth: " Here be rules. I know but one —
To dash against mine enemy and to win.   1320
Yet have I watch'd thee victor in the joust,
And seen thy way." " Heaven help thee! " sigh'd
   Lynette.

  Then for a space, and under cloud that grew
To thunder-gloom palling all stars, they rode
In converse till she made her palfrey halt,   1325
Lifted an arm, and softly whisper'd, "There."
And all the three were silent seeing, pitch'd
Beside the Castle Perilous on flat field,
A huge pavilion like a mountain peak
Sunder the glooming crimson on the marge,   1330
Black, with black banner, and a long black horn
Beside it hanging; which Sir Gareth graspt,
And so, before the two could hinder him,
Sent all his heart and breath thro' all the horn.
Echo'd the walls; a light twinkled; anon   1335
Came lights and lights, and once again he blew;
Whereon were hollow tramplings up and down
And muffled voices heard, and shadows past;
Till high above him, circled with her maids,
The Lady Lyonors at a window stood,   1340
Beautiful among lights, and waving to him
White hands and courtesy; but when the prince
Three times had blown — after long hush — at last —
The huge pavilion slowly yielded up,
Thro' those black foldings, that which housed therein.
High on a night-black horse, in night-black arms, 1346

With white breast-bone, and barren ribs of Death,
And crown'd with fleshless laughter — some ten
    steps —
In the half-light — thro' the dim dawn — advanced
The monster, and then paused, and spake no word. 1350

  But Gareth spake and all indignantly:
"Fool, for thou hast, men say, the strength of ten,
Canst thou not trust the limbs thy God hath given,
But must, to make the terror of thee more,
Trick thyself out in ghastly imageries   1355
Of that which Life hath done with, and the clod,
Less dull than thou, will hide with mantling flowers
As if for pity?" But he spake no word;
Which set the horror higher: a maiden swoon'd;
The Lady Lyonors wrung her hands and wept,   1360
As doom'd to be the bride of Night and Death;
Sir Gareth's head prickled beneath his helm;
And even Sir Lancelot thro' his warm blood felt
Ice strike, and all that mark'd him were aghast.

  At once Sir Lancelot's charger fiercely neigh'd, 1365
And Death's dark war-horse bounded forward with
    him.
Then those that did not blink the terror saw
That Death was cast to ground, and slowly rose.
But with one stroke Sir Gareth split the skull.
Half fell to right and half to left and lay.   1370
Then with a stronger buffet he clove the helm
As throughly as the skull; and out from this
Issued the bright face of a blooming boy
Fresh as a flower new-born, and crying, "Knight,
Slay me not: my three brethren bade me do it,   1375
To make a horror all about the house,

And stay the world from Lady Lyonors;
They never dream'd the passes would be past."
Answer'd Sir Gareth graciously to one
Not many a moon his younger, " My fair child,   1380
What madness made thee challenge the chief knight
Of Arthur's hall ? " "Fair Sir, they bade me do it.
They hate the King and Lancelot, the King's friend;
They hoped to slay him somewhere on the stream,
They never dream'd the passes could be past."   1385

Then sprang the happier day from underground;
And Lady Lyonors and her house, with dance
And revel and song, made merry over Death,
As being after all their foolish fears
And horrors only proven a blooming boy.   1390
So large mirth lived, and Gareth won the quest.

And he that told the tale in older times
Says that Sir Gareth wedded Lyonors,
But he that told it later says Lynette.

LANCELOT AND ELAINE

Elaine the fair, Elaine the lovable,
Elaine, the lily maid of Astolat,
High in her chamber up a tower to the east
Guarded the sacred shield of Lancelot;
Which first she placed where morning's earliest ray 5
Might strike it, and awake her with the gleam;
Then fearing rust or soilure fashion'd for it
A case of silk, and braided thereupon
All the devices blazon'd on the shield
In their own tint, and added, of her wit, 10
A border fantasy of branch and flower,
And yellow-throated nestling in the nest.
Nor rested thus content, but day by day,
Leaving her household and good father, climb'd
That eastern tower, and entering barr'd her door, 15
Stript off the case, and read the naked shield,
Now guess'd a hidden meaning in his arms,
Now made a pretty history to herself
Of every dint a sword had beaten in it,
And every scratch a lance had made upon it, 20
Conjecturing when and where: this cut is fresh;
That ten years back; this dealt him at Caerlyle;
That at Caerleon; this at Camelot:
And ah God's mercy, what a stroke was there!
And here a thrust that might have kill'd, but God 25
Broke the strong lance, and roll'd his enemy down,
And saved him: so she lived in fantasy.

How came the lily maid by that good shield
Of Lancelot, she that knew not ev'n his name?

He left it with her, when he rode to tilt   30
For the great diamond in the diamond jousts,
Which Arthur had ordain'd, and by that name
Had named them, since a diamond was the prize.

    For Arthur, long before they crown'd him King,
Roving the trackless realms of Lyonnesse,   35
Had found a glen, gray boulder and black tarn.
A horror lived about the tarn, and clave
Like its own mists to all the mountain side.
For here two brothers, one a king, had met,
And fought together; but their names were lost;   40
And each had slain his brother at a blow;
And down they fell and made the glen abhorr'd:
And there they lay till all their bones were bleach'd,
And lichen'd into color with the crags:
And he, that once was king, had on a crown   45
Of diamonds, one in front and four aside.
And Arthur came, and laboring up the pass,
All in a misty moonshine, unawares
Had trodden that crown'd skeleton, and the skull
Brake from the nape, and from the skull the crown 50
Roll'd into light, and turning on its rims
Fled like a glittering rivulet to the tarn:
And down the shingly scaur he plunged, and caught,
And set it on his head, and in his heart
Heard murmurs, "Lo, thou likewise shalt be King." 55

    Thereafter, when a King, he had the gems
Pluck'd from the crown, and show'd them to his knights,
Saying, "These jewels, whereupon I chanced
Divinely, are the kingdom's, not the King's —
For public use: henceforward let there be,   60
Once every year, a joust for one of these:

For so by nine years' proof we needs must learn
Which is our mightiest, and ourselves shall grow
In use of arms and manhood, till we drive
The heathen, who, some say, shall rule the land   65
Hereafter, which God hinder." Thus he spoke:
And eight years past, eight jousts had been, and
     still
Had Lancelot won the diamond of the year,
With purpose to present them to the Queen,
When all were won; but meaning all at once   70
To snare her royal fancy with a boon
Worth half her realm, had never spoken word.

Now for the central diamond and the last
And largest, Arthur, holding then his court
Hard on the river nigh the place which now   75
Is this world's hugest, let proclaim a joust
At Camelot, and when the time drew nigh
Spake (for she had been sick) to Guinevere,
"Are you so sick, my Queen, you cannot move
To these fair jousts?" "Yea, lord," she said, "ye
     know it."   80
"Then will ye miss," he answer'd, "the great deeds
Of Lancelot, and his prowess in the lists,
A sight ye love to look on." And the Queen
Lifted her eyes, and they dwelt languidly
On Lancelot, where he stood beside the King.   85
He thinking that he read her meaning there,
"Stay with me, I am sick; my love is more
Than many diamonds," yielded; and a heart
Love-loyal to the least wish of the Queen
(However much he yearn'd to make complete   90
The tale of diamonds for his destined boon)
Urged him to speak against the truth, and say,

" Sir King, mine ancient wound is hardly whole,
And lets me from the saddle ; " and the King
Glanced first at him, then her, and went his way.   95
No sooner gone than suddenly she began :

" To blame, my lord Sir Lancelot, much to blame!
Why go ye not to these fair jousts ? the knights
Are half of them our enemies, and the crowd
Will murmur, ' Lo, the shameless ones, who take   100
Their pastime now the trustful King is gone ! ' "
Then Lancelot vext at having lied in vain :
" Are ye so wise ? ye were not once so wise,
My Queen, that summer, when ye loved me first.
Then of the crowd ye took no more account   105
Than of the myriad cricket of the mead,
When its own voice clings to each blade of grass,
And every voice is nothing. As to knights,
Them surely I can silence with all ease.
But now my loyal worship is allow'd   110
Of all men : many a bard, without offence,
Has link'd our names together in his lay,
Lancelot, the flower of bravery, Guinevere,
The pearl of beauty : and our knights at feast
Have pledged us in this union, while the King   115
Would listen smiling. How then ? is there more ?
Has Arthur spoken aught ? or would yourself,
Now weary of my service and devoir,
Henceforth be truer to your faultless lord ? "

She broke into a little scornful laugh :   120
" Arthur, my lord, Arthur, the faultless King,
That passionate perfection, my good lord —
But who can gaze upon the Sun in heaven ?
He never spake a word of reproach to me,

He never had a glimpse of mine untruth,   125
He cares not for me : only here to-day
There gleam'd a vague suspicion in his eyes :
Some meddling rogue has tamper'd with him — else
Rapt in this fancy of his Table Round,
And swearing men to vows impossible,   130
To make them like himself : but, friend, to me
He is all fault who has no fault at all :
For who loves me must have a touch of earth ;
The low sun makes the color : I am yours,
Not Arthur's, as ye know, save by the bond.   135
And therefore hear my words : go to the jousts :
The tiny-trumpeting gnat can break our dream
When sweetest ; and the vermin voices here
May buzz so loud — we scorn them, but they sting."

    Then answer'd Lancelot, the chief of knights :   140
" And with what face, after my pretext made,
Shall I appear, O Queen, at Camelot, I
Before a King who honors his own word,
As if it were his God's ? "

                        " Yea," said the Queen,
" A moral child without the craft to rule,   145
Else had he not lost me : but listen to me,
If I must find you wit : we hear it said
That men go down before your spear at a touch,
But knowing you are Lancelot ; your great name,
This conquers : hide it therefore ; go unknown :   150
Win ! by this kiss you will : and our true King
Will then allow your pretext, O my knight,
As all for glory ; for to speak him true,
Ye know right well, how meek soe'er he seem,
No keener hunter after glory breathes.   155

He loves it in his knights more than himself:
They prove to him his work: win and return."

Then got Sir Lancelot suddenly to horse,
Wroth at himself. Not willing to be known,
He left the barren-beaten thoroughfare,   160
Chose the green path that show'd the rarer foot,
And there among the solitary downs,
Full often lost in fancy, lost his way;
Till as he traced a faintly-shadow'd track,
That all in loops and links among the dales   165
Ran to the Castle of Astolat, he saw
Fired from the west, far on a hill, the towers.
Thither he made, and blew the gateway horn.
Then came an old, dumb, myriad-wrinkled man
Who let him into lodging and disarm'd.   170
And Lancelot marvell'd at the wordless man;
And issuing found the Lord of Astolat
With two strong sons, Sir Torre and Sir Lavaine,
Moving to meet him in the castle court;
And close behind them stept the lily maid   175
Elaine, his daughter: mother of the house
There was not: some light jest among them rose
With laughter dying down as the great knight
Approach'd them: then the Lord of Astolat:
" Whence comest thou, my guest, and by what name 180
Livest between the lips? for by thy state
And presence I might guess the chief of those,
After the King, who eat in Arthur's halls.
Him have I seen: the rest, his Table Round,
Known as they are, to me they are unknown."   185

Then answer'd Lancelot, the chief of knights:
" Known am I, and of Arthur's hall, and known,

What I by mere mischance have brought, my shield,
But since I go to joust as one unknown
At Camelot for the diamond, ask me not,   190
Hereafter ye shall know me — and the shield —
I pray you lend me one, if such you have,
Blank, or at least with some device not mine."

Then said the Lord of Astolat, " Here is Torre's:
Hurt in his first tilt was my son, Sir Torre ;   195
And so, God wot, his shield is blank enough.
His ye can have." Then added plain Sir Torre,
" Yea, since I cannot use it, ye may have it."
Here laughed the father saying, " Fie, Sir Churl,
Is that an answer for a noble knight?   200
Allow him ! but Lavaine, my younger here,
He is so full of lustlihood, he will ride,
Joust for it, and win, and bring it in an hour,
And set it in this damsel's golden hair,
To make her thrice as wilful as before."   205

" Nay, father, nay, good father, shame me not
Before this noble knight," said young Lavaine,
" For nothing. Surely I but play'd on Torre:
He seem'd so sullen, vext he could not go :
A jest, no more ! for, knight, the maiden dreamt   210
That some one put this diamond in her hand,
And that it was too slippery to be held,
And slipt and fell into some pool or stream,
The castle-well, belike ; and then I said
That *if* I went and *if* I fought and won it   215
(But all was jest and joke among ourselves)
Then must she keep it safelier. All was jest.
But, father, give me leave, an if he will,
To ride to Camelot with this noble knight:

Win shall I not, but do my best to win: 220
Young as I am, yet would I do my best."

"So ye will grace me," answer'd Lancelot,
Smiling a moment, "with your fellowship
O'er these waste downs whereon I lost myself,
Then were I glad of you as guide and friend: 225
And you shall win this diamond — as I hear,
It is a fair large diamond, — if ye may,
And yield it to this maiden, if ye will."
"A fair large diamond," added plain Sir Torre,
"Such be for queens, and not for simple maids."   230
Then she who held her eyes upon the ground,
Elaine, and heard her name so tost about,
Flush'd slightly at the slight disparagement
Before the stranger knight, who, looking at her,
Full courtly, yet not falsely, thus return'd: 235
"If what is fair be but for what is fair,
And only queens are to be counted so,
Rash were my judgment then, who deem this maid
Might wear as fair a jewel as is on earth,
Not violating the bond of like to like."   240

He spoke and ceased: the lily maid Elaine,
Won by the mellow voice before she look'd,
Lifted her eyes, and read his lineaments.
The great and guilty love he bare the Queen,
In battle with the love he bare his lord,   245
Had marr'd his face, and mark'd it ere his time.
Another sinning on such heights with one,
The flower of all the west and all the world,
Had been the sleeker for it; but in him
His mood was often like a fiend, and rose   250
And drove him into wastes and solitudes

For agony, who was yet a living soul.
Marr'd as he was, he seem'd the goodliest man
That ever among ladies ate in hall,
And noblest, when she lifted up her eyes.   255
However marr'd, of more than twice her years,
Seam'd with an ancient swordcut on the cheek,
And bruised and bronzed, she lifted up her eyes
And loved him, with that love which was her doom.

Then the great knight, the darling of the court, 260
Loved of the loveliest, into that rude hall
Stept with all grace, and not with half disdain
Hid under grace, as in a smaller time,
But kindly man moving among his kind:
Whom they with meats and vintage of their best, 265
And talk and minstrel melody entertain'd.
And much they ask'd of court and Table Round,
And ever well and readily answer'd he:
But Lancelot, when they glanced at Guinevere,
Suddenly speaking of the wordless man,   270
Heard from the Baron that, ten years before,
The heathen caught and reft him of his tongue.
"He learnt and warn'd me of their fierce design
Against my house, and him they caught and maim'd;
But I, my sons, and little daughter fled   275
From bonds or death, and dwelt among the woods
By the great river in a boatman's hut.
Dull days were those, till our good Arthur broke
The Pagan yet once more on Badon hill."

"O there, great lord, doubtless," Lavaine said,
          rapt   280
By all the sweet and sudden passion of youth
Toward greatness in its elder, "you have fought.

O tell us — for we live apart — you know
Of Arthur's glorious wars." And Lancelot spoke
And answer'd him at full, as having been   285
With Arthur in the fight which all day long
Rang by the white mouth of the violent Glem;
And in the four loud battles by the shore
Of Duglas; that on Bassa; then the war
That thunder'd in and out the gloomy skirts   290
Of Celidon the forest: and again
By castle Gurnion, where the glorious King
Had on his cuirass worn our Lady's Head,
Carved of one emerald center'd in a sun
Of silver rays, that lighten'd as he breathed;   295
And at Caerleon had he help'd his lord,
When the strong neighings of the wild White Horse
Set every gilded parapet shuddering;
And up in Agned-Cathregonion too,
And down the waste sand-shores of Trath Treroit,   300
Where many a heathen fell; " and on the mount
Of Badon I myself beheld the King
Charge at the head of all his Table Round,
And all his legions crying Christ and him,
And break them; and I saw him, after, stand   305
High on a heap of slain, from spur to plume
Red as the rising sun with heathen blood,
And seeing me, with a great voice he cried,
'They are broken, they are broken!' for the King
However mild he seems at home, nor cares   310
For triumph in our mimic wars, the jousts —
For if his own knight cast him down, he laughs,
Saying, his knights are better men than he —
Yet in this heathen war the fire of God
Fills him: I never saw his like: there lives   315
No greater leader."

While he uttered this
Low to her own heart said the lily maid,
" Save your great self, fair lord " : and when he fell
From talk of war to traits of pleasantry —
Being mirthful he, but in a stately kind —   320
She still took note that when the living smile
Died from his lips, across him came a cloud
Of melancholy severe, from which again,
Whenever in her hovering to and fro
The lily maid had striven to make him cheer,   325
There brake a sudden-beaming tenderness
Of manners and of nature: and she thought
That all was nature, all, perchance, for her.
And all night long his face before her lived,
As when a painter, poring on a face,   330
Divinely thro' all hindrance finds the man
Behind it and so paints him that his face,
The shape and color of a mind and life,
Lives for his children, ever at its best
And fullest; so the face before her lived,   335
Dark-splendid, speaking in the silence, full
Of noble things, and held her from her sleep.
Till rathe she rose, half-cheated in the thought
She needs must bid farewell to sweet Lavaine.
First as in fear, step after step, she stole   340
Down the long tower-stairs, hesitating :
Anon, she heard Sir Lancelot cry in the court,
" This shield, my friend, where is it ? " and Lavaine
Past inward, as she came from out the tower.
There to his proud horse Lancelot turn'd, and smooth'd
The glossy shoulder, humming to himself.   346
Half-envious of the flattering hand, she drew
Nearer and stood. He look'd, and more amazed
Than if seven men had set upon him, saw

The maiden standing in the dewy light. 350
He had not dream'd she was so beautiful.
Then came on him a sort of sacred fear,
For silent, tho' he greeted her, she stood
Rapt on his face as if it were a god's.
Suddenly flash'd on her a wild desire, 355
That he should wear her favor at the tilt.
She braved a riotous heart in asking for it.

"Fair lord, whose name I know not — noble it is,
I well believe, the noblest — will you wear
My favor at this tourney?" "Nay," said he, 360
"Fair lady, since I never yet have worn
Favor of any lady in the lists.
Such is my wont, as those who know me know."
"Yea, so," she answer'd; "then in wearing mine
Needs must be lesser likelihood, noble lord, 365
That those who know should know you." And he turn'd
Her counsel up and down within his mind,
And found it true, and answer'd: "True, my child.
Well, I will wear it: fetch it out to me:
What is it?" and she told him "A red sleeve 370
Broider'd with pearls," and brought it: then he bound
Her token on his helmet, with a smile,
Saying, "I never yet have done so much
For any maiden living," and the blood
Sprang to her face and fill'd her with delight; 375
But left her all the paler, when Lavaine
Returning brought the yet-unblazon'd shield,
His brother's; which he gave to Lancelot,
Who parted with his own to fair Elaine:
"Do me this grace, my child, to have my shield 380
In keeping till I come." "A grace to me,"
She answer'd, "twice to-day. I am your squire!"

Whereat Lavaine said, laughing, " Lily maid,
For fear our people call you lily maid
In earnest, let me bring your color back;   385
Once, twice, and thrice: now get you hence to bed."
So kiss'd her, and Sir Lancelot his own hand,
And thus they moved away: she stay'd a minute,
Then made a sudden step to the gate, and there —
Her bright hair blown about the serious face   390
Yet rosy-kindled with her brother's kiss —
Paused by the gateway, standing near the shield
In silence, while she watch'd their arms far-off
Sparkle, until they dipt below the downs.
Then to her tower she climb'd, and took the shield, 395
There kept it, and so lived in fantasy.

Meanwhile the new companions past away
Far o'er the long backs of the bushless downs,
To where Sir Lancelot knew there lived a knight
Not far from Camelot, now for forty years   400
A hermit, who had pray'd, labor'd and pray'd,
And ever laboring had scoop'd himself
In the white rock a chapel and a hall
On massive columns, like a shorecliff cave,
And cells and chambers: all were fair and dry;   405
The green light from the meadows underneath
Struck up and lived along the milky roofs;
And in the meadows tremulous aspen-trees
And poplars made a noise of falling showers.
And thither wending there that night they bode.   410

But when the next day broke from underground,
And shot red fire and shadows thro' the cave,
They rose, heard mass, broke fast, and rode away:
Then Lancelot saying, " Hear, but hold my name

Hidden, you ride with Lancelot of the Lake,"   415
Abash'd Lavaine, whose instant reverence,
Dearer to true young hearts than their own praise,
But left him leave to stammer, " Is it indeed ? "
And after muttering "The great Lancelot,"
At last he got his breath and answer'd, " One,   420
One have I seen — that other, our liege lord,
The dread Pendragon, Britain's King of kings,
Of whom the people talk mysteriously,
He will be there — then were I stricken blind
That minute, I might say that I had seen."   425

So spake Lavaine, and when they reach'd the lists
By Camelot in the meadow, let his eyes
Run thro' the peopled gallery which half round
Lay like a rainbow fall'n upon the grass,
Until they found the clear-faced King, who sat   430
Robed in red samite, easily to be known,
Since to his crown the golden dragon clung,
And down his robe the dragon writhed in gold,
And from the carven-work behind him crept
Two dragons gilded, sloping down to make   435
Arms for his chair, while all the rest of them
Thro' knots and loops and folds innumerable
Fled ever thro' the woodwork, till they found
The new design wherein they lost themselves,
Yet with all ease, so tender was the work: 440
And, in the costly canopy o'er him set,
Blazed the last diamond of the nameless king.

Then Lancelot answer'd young Lavaine and said,
" Me you call great: mine is the firmer seat,
The truer lance: but there is many a youth   445
Now crescent, who will come to all I am

And overcome it; and in me there dwells
No greatness, save it be some far-off touch
Of greatness to know well I am not great:
There is the man." And Lavaine gaped upon him 450
As on a thing miraculous, and anon
The trumpets blew; and then did either side,
They that assail'd, and they that held the lists,
Set lance in rest, strike spur, suddenly move,
Meet in the midst, and there so furiously   455
Shock, that a man far-off might well perceive,
If any man that day were left afield,
The hard earth shake, and a low thunder of arms.
And Lancelot bode a little, till he saw
Which were the weaker; then he hurl'd into it   460
Against the stronger: little need to speak
Of Lancelot in his glory! King, duke, earl,
Count, baron — whom he smote, he overthrew.

But in the field were Lancelot's kith and kin,
Ranged with the Table Round that held the lists, 465
Strong men, and wrathful that a stranger knight
Should do and almost overdo the deeds
Of Lancelot and one said to the other, "Lo!
What is he? I do not mean the force alone —
The grace and versatility of the man!   470
Is it not Lancelot?" "When has Lancelot worn
Favor of any lady in the lists?
Not such his wont, as we that know him know."
"How then? who then?" a fury seized them all,
A fiery family passion for the name   475
Of Lancelot, and a glory one with theirs.
They couch'd their spears and prick'd their steeds,
      and thus
Their plumes driv'n backward by the wind they made

In moving, all together down upon him
Bare, as a wild wave in the wide North-sea,   480
Green-glimmering toward the summit, bears, with all
Its stormy crests that smoke against the skies,
Down on a bark, and overbears the bark,
And him that helms it, so they overbore
Sir Lancelot and his charger, and a spear   485
Down-glancing lamed the charger, and a spear
Prick'd sharply his own cuirass, and the head
Pierced thro' his side, and there snapt, and remain'd.

Then Sir Lavaine did well and worshipfully;
He bore a knight of old repute to the earth,   490
And brought his horse to Lancelot where he lay.
He up the side, sweating with agony, got,
But thought to do while he might yet endure,
And being lustily holpen by the rest,
His party, — tho' it seem'd half-miracle   495
To those he fought with, — drave his kith and kin,
And all the Table Round that held the lists,
Back to the barrier; then the trumpets blew
Proclaiming his the prize, who wore the sleeve
Of scarlet, and the pearls; and all the knights,   500
His party, cried " Advance and take thy prize
The diamond;" but he answer'd, " Diamond me
No diamonds! for God's love, a little air!
Prize me no prizes, for my prize is death!
Hence will I, and I charge you follow me not."   505

He spoke, and vanish'd suddenly from the field
With young Lavaine into the poplar grove.
There from his charger down he slid, and sat,
Gasping to Sir Lavaine, " Draw the lance-head:"
" Ah my sweet lord Sir Lancelot," said Lavaine,   510

"I dread me, if I draw it, you will die."
But he, "I die already with it: draw —
Draw," — and Lavaine drew, and Sir Lancelot gave
A marvellous great shriek and ghastly groan,
And half his blood burst forth, and down he sank 515
For the pure pain, and wholly swoon'd away.
Then came the hermit out and bare him in,
There stanch'd his wound; and there, in daily doubt
Whether to live or die, for many a week
Hid from the wide world's rumor by the grove 520
Of poplars with their noise of falling showers,
And ever-tremulous aspen-trees, he lay.

But on that day when Lancelot fled the lists,
His party, knights of utmost North and West,
Lords of waste marches, kings of desolate isles, 525
Came round their great Pendragon, saying to him,
"Lo, Sire, our knight, thro' whom we won the day,
Hath gone sore wounded, and hath left his prize
Untaken, crying that his prize is death."
"Heaven hinder," said the King, "that such an one, 530
So great a knight as we have seen to-day —
He seem'd to me another Lancelot —
Yea, twenty times I thought him Lancelot —
He must not pass uncared for. Wherefore, rise,
O Gawain, and ride forth and find the knight. 535
Wounded and wearied, needs must he be near.
I charge you that you get at once to horse.
And, knights and kings, there breathes not one of you
Will deem this prize of ours is rashly given:
His prowess was too wondrous. We will do him 540
No customary honor: since the knight
Came not to us, of us to claim the prize,
Ourselves will send it after. Rise and take

This diamond, and deliver it, and return,
And bring us where he is, and how he fares,   545
And cease not from your quest until ye find."

   So saying, from the carven flower above,
To which it made a restless heart, he took,
And gave, the diamond; then from where he sat
At Arthur's right, with smiling face arose,   550
With smiling face and frowning heart, a Prince
In the mid might and flourish of his May,
Gawain, surnamed The Courteous, fair and strong,
And after Lancelot, Tristram, and Geraint
And Gareth, a good knight, but therewithal   555
Sir Modred's brother, and the child of Lot,
Nor often loyal to his word, and now
Wroth that the King's command to sally forth
In quest of whom he knew not, made him leave
The banquet, and concourse of knights and kings.   560

   So all in wrath he got to horse and went;
While Arthur to the banquet, dark in mood,
Past, thinking, "Is it Lancelot who hath come
Despite the wound he spake of, all for gain
Of glory, and hath added wound to wound,   565
And ridd'n away to die?" So feared the King,
And, after two days' tarriance there, return'd.
Then when he saw the Queen, embracing ask'd,
"Love, are you yet so sick?" "Nay, lord," she said.
"And where is Lancelot?" Then the Queen amazed, 570
"Was he not with you? won he not your prize?"
"Nay, but one like him." "Why that like was he."
And when the King demanded how she knew,
Said, "Lord, no sooner had ye parted from us,
Than Lancelot told me of a common talk   575

That men went down before his spear at a touch,
But knowing he was Lancelot; his great name
Conquer'd; and therefore would he hide his name
From all men, ev'n the King, and to this end
Had made the pretext of a hindering wound, 580
That he might joust unknown of all, and learn
If his old prowess were in aught decay'd;
And added, 'Our true Arthur, when he learns,
Will well allow my pretext, as for gain
Of purer glory.'"

                 Then replied the King: 585
"Far lovelier in our Lancelot had it been,
In lieu of idly dallying with the truth,
To have trusted me as he hath trusted thee.
Surely his King and most familiar friend
Might well have kept his secret. True, indeed, 590
Albeit I know my knights fantastical,
So fine a fear in our large Lancelot
Must needs have moved my laughter : now remains
But little cause for laughter : his own kin —
Ill news, my Queen, for all who love him, this ! — 595
His kith and kin, not knowing, set upon him ;
So that he went sore wounded from the field :
Yet good news too : for goodly hopes are mine
That Lancelot is no more a lonely heart.
He wore, against his wont, upon his helm 600
A sleeve of scarlet, broider'd with great pearls,
Some gentle maiden's gift."

                      "Yea, lord," she said,
"Thy hopes are mine," and saying that, she choked,
And sharply turn'd about to hide her face,
Past to her chamber, and there flung herself 605

Down on the great King's couch, and writhed upon it,
And clench'd her fingers till they bit the palm,
And shriek'd out " Traitor ! " to the unhearing wall,
Then flash'd into wild tears, and rose again,
And moved about her palace, proud and pale.   610

Gawain the while thro' all the region round
Rode with his diamond, wearied of the quest,
Touch'd at all points, except the poplar grove,
And came at last, tho' late, to Astolat:
Whom glittering in enamell'd arms the maid   615
Glanced at, and cried, " What news from Camelot, lord?
What of the knight with the red sleeve ? "   " He won."
" I knew it," she said.   " But parted from the jousts
Hurt in the side," whereat she caught her breath ;
Thro' her own side she felt the sharp lance go ;   620
Thereon she smote her hand ; wellnigh she swoon'd ;
And, while he gazed wonderingly at her, came
The Lord of Astolat out, to whom the Prince
Reported who he was, and on what quest
Sent, that he bore the prize and could not find   625
The victor, but had ridd'n a random round
To seek him, and had wearied of the search.
To whom the Lord of Astolat, " Bide with us,
And ride no more at random, noble Prince !
Here was the knight, and here he left a shield ;   630
This will he send or come for: furthermore
Our son is with him ; we shall hear anon,
Needs must we hear."   To this the courteous Prince
Accorded with his wonted courtesy,
Courtesy with a touch of traitor in it,   635
And stay'd ; and cast his eyes on fair Elaine:
Where could be found face daintier ? then her shape,
From forehead down to foot, perfect — again

From foot to forehead exquisitely turn'd:
" Well — if I bide, lo! this wild flower for me!" 640
And oft they met among the garden yews,
And there he set himself to play upon her
With sallying wit, free flashes from a height
Above her, graces of the court, and songs,
Sighs, and slow smiles, and golden eloquence 645
And amorous adulation, till the maid
Rebell'd against it, saying to him, " Prince,
O loyal nephew of our noble King,
Why ask you not to see the shield he left,
Whence you might learn his name? Why slight
        your King 650
And lose the quest he sent you on, and prove
No surer than our falcon yesterday,
Who lost the hern we slipt her at, and went
To all the winds?" "Nay, by mine head," said he,
" I lose it, as we lose the lark in heaven, 655
O damsel, in the light of your blue eyes;
But an ye will it let me see the shield."
And when the shield was brought, and Gawain saw
Sir Lancelot's azure lions, crown'd with gold,
Ramp in the field, he smote his thigh, and mock'd: 660
" Right was the King! our Lancelot! that true man!"
" And right was I," she answer'd merrily, " I,
Who dream'd my knight the greatest knight of all."
" And if *I* dream'd," said Gawain, " that you love
This greatest knight, your pardon! lo, ye know it! 665
Speak therefore: shall I waste myself in vain?"
Full simple was her answer, " What know I?
My brethren have been all my fellowship;
And I, when often they have talk'd of love,
Wish'd it had been my mother, for they talk'd, 670
Meseem'd, of what they knew not; so myself —

I know not if I know what true love is,
But if I know, then, if I love not him,
I know there is none other I can love."
"Yea, by God's death," said he, "ye love him well,
But would not, knew ye what all others know,   676
And whom he loves." "So be it," cried Elaine,
And lifted her fair face and moved away:
But he pursued her, calling, "Stay a little!
One golden minute's grace! he wore your sleeve: 680
Would he break faith with one I may not name?
Must our true man change like a leaf at last?
Nay — like enow: why then, far be it from me
To cross our mighty Lancelot in his loves!
And, damsel, for I deem you know full well   685
Where your great knight is hidden, let me leave
My quest with you; the diamond also: here!
For if you love, it will be sweet to give it;
And if he love, it will be sweet to have it
From your own hand; and whether he love or not,   690
A diamond is a diamond. Fare you well
A thousand times! — a thousand times farewell!
Yet, if he love, and his love hold, we two
May meet at court hereafter: there, I think,
So ye will learn the courtesies of the court,   695
We two shall know each other."

                                   Then he gave,
And slightly kiss'd the hand to which he gave,
The diamond, and all wearied of the quest
Leapt on his horse, and carolling as he went
A true-love ballad, lightly rode away.   700

   Thence to the court he past; there told the King
What the King knew, "Sir Lancelot is the knight."

And added, "Sire, my liege, so much I learnt;
But fail'd to find him tho' I rode all round
The region: but I lighted on the maid   705
Whose sleeve he wore; she loves him: and to her,
Deeming our courtesy is the truest law,
I gave the diamond: she will render it;
For by mine head she knows his hiding-place."

    The seldom-frowning King frown'd, and replied, 710
"Too courteous truly! ye shall go no more
On quest of mine, seeing that ye forget
Obedience is the courtesy due to kings."

    He spake and parted. Wroth, but all in awe,
For twenty strokes of the blood, without a word, 715
Linger'd that other, staring after him;
Then shook his hair, strode off, and buzz'd abroad
About the maid of Astolat, and her love.
All ears were prick'd at once, all tongues were loosed:
"The maid of Astolat loves Sir Lancelot,   720
Sir Lancelot loves the maid of Astolat."
Some read the King's face, some the Queen's, and all
Had marvel what the maid might be, but most
Predoom'd her as unworthy. One old dame
Came suddenly on the Queen with the sharp news. 725
She, that had heard the noise of it before,
But sorrowing Lancelot should have stoop'd so low,
Marr'd her friend's aim with pale tranquillity.
So ran the tale like fire about the court,
Fire in dry stubble a nine-days' wonder flared: 730
Till ev'n the knights at banquet twice or thrice
Forgot to drink to Lancelot and the Queen,
And pledging Lancelot and the lily maid
Smiled at each other, while the Queen, who sat

With lips severely placid, felt the knot   735
Climb in her throat, and with her feet unseen
Crush'd the wild passion out against the floor
Beneath the banquet, where the meats became
As wormwood, and she hated all who pledged.

But far away the maid in Astolat,   740
Her guiltless rival, she that ever kept
The one-day-seen Sir Lancelot in her heart,
Crept to her father, while he mused alone,
Sat on his knee, stroked his gray face and said,
"Father, you call me wilful, and the fault   745
Is yours who let me have my will, and now,
Sweet father, will you let me lose my wits?"
"Nay," said he, "surely." "Wherefore, let me hence,"
She answer'd, "and find out our dear Lavaine."
"Ye will not lose your wits for dear Lavaine: 750
Bide," answer'd he: "we needs must hear anon
Of him, and of that other." "Ay," she said,
"And of that other, for I needs must hence
And find that other, wheresoe'er he be,
And with mine own hand give his diamond to him,   755
Lest I be found as faithless in the quest
As yon proud Prince who left the quest to me.
Sweet father, I behold him in my dreams
Gaunt as it were the skeleton of himself,
Death-pale, for lack of gentle maiden's aid.   760
The gentler-born the maiden, the more bound,
My father, to be sweet and serviceable
To noble knights in sickness, as ye know,
When these have worn their tokens: let me hence,
I pray you." Then her father nodding said,   765
"Ay, ay, the diamond: wit ye well, my child,
Right fain were I to learn this knight were whole,

Being our greatest: yea, and you must give it—
And sure I think this fruit is hung too high
For any mouth to gape for save a queen's—   770
Nay, I mean nothing: so then, get you gone,
Being so very wilful you must go."

Lightly, her suit allow'd, she slipt away,
And while she made her ready for her ride,
Her father's latest word humm'd in her ear,   775
"Being so very wilful you must go,"
And changed itself and echo'd in her heart,
"Being so very wilful you must die."
But she was happy enough and shook it off,
As we shake off the bee that buzzes at us;   780
And in her heart she answer'd it and said,
"What matter, so I help him back to life?"
Then far away with good Sir Torre for guide
Rode o'er the long backs of the bushless downs
To Camelot, and before the city-gates   785
Came on her brother with a happy face
Making a roan horse caper and curvet
For pleasure all about a field of flowers:
Whom when she saw, "Lavaine," she cried, "Lavaine,
How fares my lord Sir Lancelot?" He amazed,   790
"Torre and Elaine! why here? Sir Lancelot?
How know ye my lord's name is Lancelot?"
But when the maid had told him all her tale,
Then turn'd Sir Torre, and being in his moods
Left them, and under the strange-statued gate,   795
Where Arthur's wars were render'd mystically,
Past up the still rich city to his kin,
His own far blood, which dwelt at Camelot;
And her Lavaine across the poplar grove
Led to the caves: there first she saw the casque   800

Of Lancelot on the wall: her scarlet sleeve,
Tho' carved and cut, and half the pearls away,
Stream'd from it still; and in her heart she laugh'd,
Because he had not loosed it from his helm,
But meant once more perchance to tourney in it.   805
And when they gain'd the cell wherein he slept,
His battle-writhen arms and mighty hands
Lay naked on the wolfskin, and a dream
Of dragging down his enemy made them move.
Then she that saw him lying unsleek, unshorn,   810
Gaunt as it were the skeleton of himself,
Utter'd a little tender dolorous cry.
The sound not wonted in a place so still
Woke the sick knight, and while he roll'd his eyes
Yet blank from sleep, she started to him, saying,   815
" Your prize the diamond sent you by the King: "
His eyes glisten'd: she fancied " Is it for me? "
And when the maid had told him all the tale
Of King and Prince, the diamond sent, the quest
Assign'd to her not worthy of it, she knelt   820
Full lowly by the corners of his bed,
And laid the diamond in his open hand.
Her face was near, and as we kiss the child
That does the task assign'd, he kiss'd her face.
At once she slipt like water to the floor.   825
" Alas," he said, " your ride hath wearied you.
Rest must you have." " No rest for me," she said;
" Nay, for near you, fair lord, I am at rest."
What might she mean by that? his large black eyes,
Yet larger thro' his leanness, dwelt upon her,   830
Till all her heart's sad secret blazed itself
In the heart's colors on her simple face;
And Lancelot look'd and was perplext in mind,
And being weak in body said no more;

But did not love the color; woman's love,   835
Save one, he not regarded, and so turn'd
Sighing, and feign'd a sleep until he slept.

Then rose Elaine and glided thro' the fields,
And past beneath the weirdly-sculptured gates
Far up the dim rich city to her kin;   840
There bode the night; but woke with dawn, and
     past
Down thro' the dim rich city to the fields,
Thence to the cave: so day by day she past
In either twilight ghost-like to and fro
Gliding, and every day she tended him,   845
And likewise many a night: and Lancelot
Would, tho' he call'd his wound a little hurt
Whereof he should be quickly whole, at times
Brain-feverous in his heat and agony, seem
Uncourteous, even he: but the meek maid   850
Sweetly forebore him ever, being to him
Meeker than any child to a rough nurse,
Milder than any mother to a sick child,
And never woman yet, since man's first fall,
Did kindlier unto man, but her deep love   855
Upbore her; till the hermit, skill'd in all
The simples and the science of that time,
Told him that her fine care had saved his life.
And the sick man forgot her simple blush,
Would call her friend and sister, sweet Elaine,   860
Would listen for her coming and regret
Her parting step, and held her tenderly,
And loved her with all love except the love
Of man and woman when they love their best,
Closest and sweetest, and had died the death   865
In any knightly fashion for her sake.

And peradventure had he seen her first
She might have made this and that other world
Another world for the sick man ; but now
The shackles of an old love straiten'd him,   870
His honor rooted in dishonor stood,
And faith unfaithful kept him falsely true.

Yet the great knight in his mid-sickness made
Full many a holy vow and pure resolve.
These, as but born of sickness, could not live ;   875
For when the blood ran lustier in him again,
Full often the bright image of one face,
Making a treacherous quiet in his heart,
Dispersed his resolution like a cloud.
Then if the maiden, while that ghostly grace   880
Beam'd on his fancy, spoke, he answer'd not,
Or short and coldly, and she knew right well
What the rough sickness meant, but what this meant
She knew not, and the sorrow dimm'd her sight,
And drave her ere her time across the the fields   885
Far into the rich city, where alone
She murmur'd, " Vain, in vain : it cannot be.
He will not love me : how then ? must I die ?"
Then as a little helpless innocent bird,
That has but one plain passage of few notes,   890
Will sing the simple passage o'er and o'er
For all an April morning, till the ear
Wearies to hear it, so the simple maid
Went half the night repeating, " Must I die ?"
And now to right she turn'd, and now to left,   895
And found no ease in turning or in rest ;
And " Him or death," she mutter'd, " death or
          him,"
Again and like a burthen, " Him or death."

But when Sir Lancelot's deadly hurt was whole,
To Astolat returning rode the three. 900
There morn by morn, arraying her sweet self
In that wherein she deem'd she look'd her best,
She came before Sir Lancelot, for she thought
" If I be loved, these are my festal robes,
If not, the victim's flowers before he fall." 905
And Lancelot ever prest upon the maid
That she should ask some goodly gift of him
For her own self or hers; " and do not shun
To speak the wish most near to your true heart;
Such service have ye done me, that I make 910
My will of yours, and Prince and Lord am I
In mine own land, and what I will I can."
Then like a ghost she lifted up her face,
But like a ghost without the power to speak.
And Lancelot saw that she withheld her wish, 915
And bode among them yet a little space
Till he should learn it; and one morn it chanced
He found her in among the garden yews,
And said, " Delay no longer, speak your wish,
Seeing I go to-day:" then out she brake: 920
" Going? and we shall never see you more.
And I must die for want of one bold word."
" Speak; that I live to hear," he said, " is yours."
Then suddenly and passionately she spoke:
" I have gone mad. I love you: let me die." 925
" Ah, sister," answer'd Lancelot, " what is this?"
And innocently extending her white arms,
" Your love," she said, " your love — to be your wife."
And Lancelot answer'd, " Had I chosen to wed,
I had been wedded earlier, sweet Elaine: 930
But now there never will be wife of mine."
" No, no," she cried, " I care not to be wife,

But to be with you still, to see your face,
To serve you, and to follow you thro' the world."
And Lancelot answer'd, " Nay, the world, the world,
All ear and eye, with such a stupid heart   936
To interpret ear and eye, and such a tongue
To blare its own interpretation — nay,
Full ill then should I quit your brother's love,
And your good father's kindness." And she said,   940
" Not to be with you, not to see your face —
Alas for me then, my good days are done."
" Nay, noble maid," he answer'd, " ten times nay!
This is not love : but love's first flash in youth,
Most common : yea, I know it of mine own self :   945
And you yourself will smile at your own self
Hereafter, when you yield your flower of life
To one more fitly yours, not thrice your age :
And then will I, for true you are and sweet,
Beyond mine old belief in womanhood,   950
More specially should your good knight be poor,
Endow you with broad land and territory,
Even the half my realm beyond the seas,
So that would make you happy : furthermore,
Ev'n to the death, as tho' ye were my blood,   955
In all your quarrels will I be your knight.
This will I do, dear damsel, for your sake,
And more than this I cannot."

                                        While he spoke
She neither blush'd nor shook, but deathly-pale
Stood grasping what was nearest, then replied :   960
" Of all this will I nothing ; " and so fell,
And thus they bore her swooning to her tower.

Then spake, to whom thro' those black walls of yew

Their talk had pierced, her father : " Ay, a flash,
I fear me, that will strike my blossom dead.   965
Too courteous are ye, fair Lord Lancelot.
I pray you use some rough discourtesy
To blunt or break her passion."

                              Lancelot said,
" That were against me : what I can I will";
And there that day remain'd and toward even   970
Sent for his shield : full meekly rose the maid,
Stript off the case, and gave the naked shield ;
Then, when she heard his horse upon the stones,
Unclasping flung the casement back, and look'd
Down on his helm, from which her sleeve had gone.
And Lancelot knew the little clinking sound ;   976
And she by tact of love was well aware
That Lancelot knew that she was looking at him.
And yet he glanced not up, nor waved his hand,
Nor bade farewell, but sadly rode away.   980
This was the one discourtesy that he used.

     So in her tower alone the maiden sat :
His very shield was gone; only the case,
Her own poor work, her empty labor, left.
But still she heard him, still his picture form'd   985
And grew between her and the pictured wall.
Then came her father, saying in low tones,
" Have comfort," whom she greeted quietly.
Then came her brethren saying, " Peace to thee,
Sweet sister," whom she answer'd with all calm.   990
But when they left her to herself again,
Death, like a friend's voice from a distant field
Approaching thro' the darkness, call'd; the owls
Wailing had power upon her, and she mixt

Her fancies with the sallow-rifted glooms   995
Of evening, and the moanings of the wind.

And in those days she made a little song,
And call'd her song "The Song of Love and Death,"
And sang it: sweetly could she make and sing.

"Sweet is true love tho' given in vain, in vain; 1000
And sweet is death, who puts an end to pain:
I know not which is sweeter, no, not I.

"Love, art thou sweet? then bitter death must be:
Love, thou art bitter; sweet is death to me.
O Love, if death be sweeter, let me die.   1005

"Sweet love, that seems not made to fade away,
Sweet death, that seems to make us loveless clay,
I know not which is sweeter, no, not I.

"I fain would follow love, if that could be;
I needs must follow death, who calls for me;   1010
Call and I follow, I follow! let me die."

High with the last line scaled her voice, and this,
All in a fiery dawning wild with wind
That shook her tower, the brothers heard, and
        thought
With shuddering, "Hark the Phantom of the house
That ever shrieks before a death," and call'd   1016
The father, and all three in hurry and fear
Ran to her, and lo! the blood-red light of dawn
Flared on her face, she shrilling, "Let me die!"

As when we dwell upon a word we know,   1020

Repeating, till the word we know so well
Becomes a wonder, and we know not why,
So dwelt the father on her face, and thought
" Is this Elaine?" till back the maiden fell,
Then gave a languid hand to each, and lay,   1025
Speaking a still good-morrow with her eyes.
At last she said, " Sweet brothers, yesternight
I seem'd a curious little maid again,
As happy as when we dwelt among the woods,
And when ye used to take me with the flood   1030
Up the great river in the boatman's boat.
Only ye would not pass beyond the cape
That has the poplar on it: there ye fixt
Your limit, oft returning with the tide.
And yet I cried because ye would not pass   1035
Beyond it, and far up the shining flood
Until we found the palace of the King.
And yet ye would not; but this night I dream'd
That I was all alone upon the flood,
And then I said, 'Now shall I have my will':   1040
And there I woke, but still the wish remain'd.
So let me hence that I may pass at last
Beyond the poplar and far up the flood,
Until I find the palace of the King.
There will I enter in among them all,   1045
And no man there will dare to mock at me;
But there the fine Gawain will wonder at me,
And there the great Sir Lancelot muse at me;
Gawain, who bade a thousand farewells to me,
Lancelot, who coldly went, nor bade me one: 1050
And there the King will know me and my love,
And there the Queen herself will pity me,
And all the gentle court will welcome me,
And after my long voyage I shall rest!"

"Peace," said her father, "O my child, ye seem 1055
Light-headed, for what force is yours to go
So far, being sick? and wherefore would ye look
On this proud fellow again, who scorns us all?"

Then the rough Torre began to heave and move
And bluster into stormy sobs and say, 1060
"I never loved him: an I meet with him,
I care not howsoever great he be,
Then will I strike at him and strike him down,
Give me good fortune, I will strike him dead,
For this discomfort he hath done the house." 1065

To whom the gentle sister made reply,
"Fret not yourself, dear brother, nor be wroth,
Seeing it is no more Sir Lancelot's fault
Not to love me, than it is mine to love
Him of all men who seems to me the highest." 1070

"'Highest?'" the father answer'd, echoing "highest"
(He meant to break the passion in her), "nay,
Daughter, I know not what you call the highest;
But this I know, for all the people know it,
He loves the Queen, and in an open shame: 1075
And she returns his love in open shame.
If this be high, what is it to be low?"

Then spake the lily maid of Astolat:
"Sweet father, all too faint and sick am I
For anger: these are slanders: never yet 1080
Was noble man but made ignoble talk.
He makes no friend who never made a foe.
But now it is my glory to have loved
One peerless, without stain: so let me pass,

My father, howsoe'er I seem to you,   1085
Not all unhappy, having loved God's best
And greatest, tho' my love had no return:
Yet, seeing you desire your child to live,
Thanks, but you work against your own desire;
For if I could believe the things you say,   1090
I should but die the sooner; wherefore cease,
Sweet father, and bid call the ghostly man
Hither, and let me shrive me clean, and die."

   So when the ghostly man had come and gone,
She, with a face bright as for sin forgiven,   1095
Besought Lavaine to write as she devised
A letter, word for word; and when he ask'd,
" Is it for Lancelot, is it for my dear lord ?
Then will I bear it gladly ;" she replied,
" For Lancelot and the Queen and all the world, 1100
But I myself must bear it." Then he wrote
The letter she devised ; which being writ
And folded, "O sweet father, tender and true,
Deny me not," she said — " ye never yet
Denied my fancies — this, however strange,   1105
My latest : lay the letter in my hand
A little ere I die, and close the hand
Upon it; I shall guard it even in death.
And when the heat is gone from out my heart,
Then take the little bed on which I died   1110
For Lancelot's love, and deck it like the Queen's
For richness, and me also like the Queen
In all I have of rich, and lay me on it.
And let there be prepared a chariot-bier
To take me to the river, and a barge   1115
Be ready on the river, clothed in black.
I go in state to court, to meet the Queen.

There surely I shall speak for mine own self,
And none of you can speak for me so well.
And therefore let our dumb old man alone   1120
Go with me, he can steer and row, and he
Will guide me to that palace, to the doors."

She ceased : her father promised ; whereupon
She grew so cheerful that they deem'd her death
Was rather in the fantasy than the blood.   1125
But ten slow mornings past, and on the eleventh
Her father laid the letter in her hand,
And closed the hand upon it, and she died.
So that day there was dole in Astolat.

But when the next sun brake from underground, 1130
Then, these two brethren slowly with bent brows
Accompanying, the sad chariot-bier
Past like a shadow thro' the field, that shone
Full-summer, to that stream whereon the barge,
Pall'd all its length in blackest samite, lay.   1135
There sat the lifelong creature of the house,
Loyal, the dumb old servitor, on deck,
Winking his eyes, and twisted all his face.
So those two brethren from the chariot took
And on the black decks laid her in her bed,   1140
Set in her hand a lily, o'er her hung
The silken case with braided blazonings,
And kiss'd her quiet brows, and saying to her
"Sister, farewell for ever," and again
"Farewell, sweet sister," parted all in tears.   1145
Then rose the dumb old servitor, and the dead,
Dar'd by the dumb, went upward with the flood —
In her right hand the lily, in her left
The letter — all her bright hair streaming down —

And all the coverlid was cloth of gold 1150
Drawn to her waist, and she herself in white
All but her face, and that clear-featured face
Was lovely, for she did not seem as dead,
But fast asleep, and lay as tho' she smiled.

That day Sir Lancelot at the palace craved 1155
Audience of Guinevere, to give at last
The price of half a realm, his costly gift,
Hard-won and hardly won with bruise and blow,
With deaths of others, and almost his own,
The nine-years fought-for diamonds: for he saw 1160
One of her house, and sent him to the Queen
Bearing his wish, whereto the Queen agreed
With such and so unmoved a majesty
She might have seem'd her statue, but that he,
Low-drooping till he wellnigh kiss'd her feet 1165
For loyal awe, saw with a sidelong eye
The shadow of some piece of pointed lace,
In the Queen's shadow, vibrate on the walls,
And parted, laughing in his courtly heart.

All in an oriel on the summer side, 1170
Vine-clad, of Arthur's palace toward the stream,
They met, and Lancelot kneeling utter'd, " Queen,
Lady, my liege, in whom I have my joy,
Take, what I had not won except for you,
These jewels, and make me happy, making them 1175
An armlet for the roundest arm on earth,
Or necklace for a neck to which the swan's
Is tawnier than her cygnet's: these are words:
Your beauty is your beauty, and I sin
In speaking, yet O grant my worship of it 1180
Words, as we grant grief tears. Such sin in words,

Perchance, we both can pardon: but, my Queen,
I hear of rumors flying thro' your court.
Our bond, as not the bond of man and wife,
Should have in it an absoluter trust   1185
To make up that defect: let rumors be:
When did not rumors fly? these, as I trust
That you trust me in your own nobleness,
I may not well believe that you believe."

While thus he spoke, half turn'd away, the Queen 1190
Brake from the vast oriel-embowering vine
Leaf after leaf, and tore, and cast them off,
Till all the place whereon she stood was green;
Then, when he ceased, in one cold passive hand
Received at once and laid aside the gems   1195
There on a table near her, and replied:

"It may be, I am quicker of belief
Than you believe me, Lancelot of the Lake.
Our bond is not the bond of man and wife.
This good is in it, whatsoe'er of ill,   1200
It can be broken easier. I for you
This many a year have done despite and wrong
To one whom ever in my heart of hearts
I did acknowledge nobler. What are these?
Diamonds for me! they had been thrice their worth 1205
Being your gift, had you not lost your own.
To loyal hearts the value of all gifts
Must vary as the giver's. Not for me!
For her! for your new fancy. Only this
Grant me, I pray you: have your joys apart.   1210
I doubt not that however changed, you keep
So much of what is graceful: and myself
Would shun to break those bounds of courtesy

In which as Arthur's Queen I move and rule:
So cannot speak my mind. An end to this!   1215
A strange one! yet I take it with Amen.
So pray you, add my diamonds to her pearls;
Deck her with these; tell her, she shines me down:
An armlet for an arm to which the Queen's
Is haggard, or a necklace for a neck   1220
O as much fairer — as a faith once fair
Was richer than these diamonds — hers not mine —
Nay, by the mother of our Lord himself,
Or hers or mine, mine now to work my will —
She shall not have them."

                Saying which she seized,   1225
And thro' the casement standing wide for heat,
Flung them, and down they flash'd, and smote the
      stream,
Then from the smitten surface flash'd, as it were,
Diamonds to meet them, and they past away.
Then while Sir Lancelot leant, in half disdain   1230
At love, life, all things, on the window ledge,
Close underneath his eyes, and right across
Where these had fallen, slowly past the barge
Whereon the lily maid of Astolat
Lay smiling, like a star in blackest night.   1235

    But the wild Queen, who saw not, burst away
To weep and wail in secret; and the barge,
On to the palace-doorway sliding, paused.
There two stood arm'd, and kept the door; to whom,
All up the marble stair, tier over tier,   1240
Were added mouths that gaped, and eyes that ask'd
"What is it?" but that oarsman's haggard face,
As hard and still as is the face that men

Shape to their fancy's eye from broken rocks
On some cliff-side, appall'd them, and they said,   1245
"He is enchanted, cannot speak — and she,
Look how she sleeps — the Fairy Queen, so fair!
Yea, but how pale! what are they? flesh and blood?
Or come to take the King to Fairyland?
For some do hold our Arthur cannot die,   1250
But that he passes into Fairyland."

While thus they babbled of the King, the King
Came girt with knights: then turn'd the tongueless
      man
From the half-face to the full eye, and rose
And pointed to the damsel, and the doors.   1255
So Arthur bade the meek Sir Percivale
And pure Sir Galahad to uplift the maid;
And reverently they bore her into hall.
Then came the fine Gawain and wonder'd at her,
And Lancelot later came and mused at her,   1260
And last the Queen herself, and pitied her:
But Arthur spied the letter in her hand,
Stoopt, took, brake seal, and read it; this was all:

"Most noble lord, Sir Lancelot of the Lake,
I, sometime call'd the maid of Astolat,   1265
Come, for you left me taking no farewell,
Hither, to take my last farewell of you.
I loved you, and my love had no return,
And therefore my true love has been my death.
And therefore to our Lady Guinevere,   127(
And to all other ladies, I make moan.
Pray for my soul, and yield me burial.
Pray for my soul thou, too, Sir Lancelot,
As thou art a knight peerless."

Thus he read:

And ever in the reading, lords and dames   1275
Wept, looking often from his face who read
To hers which lay so silent, and at times,
So touch'd were they, half-thinking that her lips,
Who had devised the letter, moved again.

Then freely spoke Sir Lancelot to them all: 1280
" My lord liege Arthur, and all ye that hear
Know that for this most gentle maiden's death,
Right heavy am I; for good she was and true,
But loved me with a love beyond all love
In woman, whomsoever I have known.   1285
Yet to be loved makes not to love again;
Not at my years, however it hold in youth.
I swear by truth and knighthood that I gave
No cause, not willingly, for such a love:
To this I call my friends in testimony,   1290
Her brethren, and her father, who himself
Besought me to be plain and blunt, and use,
To break her passion, some discourtesy
Against my nature: what I could, I did.
I left her and I bade her no farewell;   1295
Tho', had I dreamt the damsel would have died,
I might have put my wits to some rough use,
And help'd her from herself."

Then said the Queen
(Sea was her wrath, yet working after storm)
" Ye might at least have done her so much grace, 1300
Fair lord, as would have help'd her from her
          death."
He raised his head, their eyes met and hers fell,
He adding:

"Queen, she would not be content
Save that I wedded her, which could not be.
Then might she follow me thro' the world, she ask'd; 1305
It could not be. I told her that her love
Was but the flash of youth, would darken down
To rise hereafter in a stiller flame
Toward one more worthy of her — then would I,
More specially were he she wedded poor,   1310
Estate them with large land and territory
In mine own realm beyond the narrow seas,
To keep them in all joyance: more than this
I could not; this she would not, and she died."

He pausing, Arthur answer'd, " O my knight, 1315
It will be to thy worship, as my knight,
And mine, as head of all our Table Round,
To see that she be buried worshipfully."

So toward that shrine which then in all the realm
Was richest, Arthur leading, slowly went   1320
The marshall'd Order of their Table Round,
And Lancelot sat beyond his wont, to see
The maiden buried, not as one unknown,
Nor meanly, but with gorgeous obsequies,
And mass, and rolling music, like a queen.   1325
And when the knights had laid her comely head
Low in the dust of half-forgotten kings,
Then Arthur spake among them, " Let her tomb
Be costly, and her image thereupon,
And let the shield of Lancelot at her feet   1330
Be carven, and her lily in her hand.
And let the story of her dolorous voyage
For all true hearts be blazon'd on her tomb
In letters gold and azure ! " which was wrought

Thereafter; but when now the lords and dames 1335
And people, from the high door streaming, brake
Disorderly, as homeward each, the Queen,
Who mark'd Sir Lancelot where he moved apart,
Drew near, and sigh'd in passing, "Lancelot,
Forgive me; mine was jealousy in love." 1340
He answer'd with his eyes upon the ground,
"That is love's curse; pass on, my Queen, forgiven."
But Arthur, who beheld his cloudy brows,
Approach'd him, and with full affection said,

"Lancelot, my Lancelot, thou in whom I have 1345
Most joy and most affiance, for I know
What thou hast been in battle by my side,
And many a time have watch'd thee at the tilt
Strike down the lusty and long-practised knight,
And let the younger and unskill'd go by 1350
To win his honor and to make his name,
And loved thy courtesies and thee, a man
Made to be loved; but now I would to God,
Seeing the homeless trouble in thine eyes,
Thou couldst have loved this maiden, shaped, it seems,
By God for thee alone, and from her face, 1356
If one may judge the living by the dead,
Delicately pure and marvellously fair,
Who might have brought thee, now a lonely man,
Wifeless and heirless, noble issue, sons 1360
Born to the glory of thy name and fame,
My knight, the great Sir Lancelot of the Lake."

Then answer'd Lancelot, "Fair she was, my King,
Pure, as you ever wish your knights to be.
To doubt her fairness were to want an eye, 1365
To doubt her pureness were to want a heart —

Yea, to be loved, if what is worthy love
Could bind him, but free love will not be bound."

"Free love, so bound, were freëst," said the King.
"Let love be free; free love is for the best: 1370
And, after heaven, on our dull side of death,
What should be best, if not so pure a love
Clothed in so pure a loveliness? yet thee
She fail'd to bind, tho' being, as I think,
Unbound as yet, and gentle, as I know."   1375

And Lancelot answer'd nothing, but he went,
And at the inrunning of a little brook
Sat by the river in a cove, and watch'd
The high reed wave, and lifted up his eyes
And saw the barge that brought her moving down,   1380
Far-off, a blot upon the stream, and said
Low in himself, "Ah simple heart and sweet,
Ye loved me, damsel, surely with a love
Far tenderer than my Queen's. Pray for thy soul?
Ay, that will I. Farewell too — now at last —   1385
Farewell, fair lily. 'Jealousy in love?'
Not rather dead love's harsh heir, jealous pride?
Queen, if I grant the jealousy as of love,
May not your crescent fear for name and fame,
Speak, as it waxes, of a love that wanes?   1390
Why did the King dwell on my name to me?
Mine own name shames me, seeming a reproach,
Lancelot, whom the Lady of the Lake
Caught from his mother's arms — the wondrous one
Who passes thro' the vision of the night —   1395
She chanted snatches of mysterious hymns
Heard on the winding waters, eve and morn.
She kiss'd me saying, 'Thou art fair, my child,

As a king's son,' and often in her arms
She bare me, pacing on the dusky mere. 1400
Would she had drown'd me in it, where'er it be!
For what am I? what profits me my name
Of greatest knight? I fought for it, and have it:
Pleasure to have it, none; to lose it, pain;
Now grown a part of me: but what use in it? 1405
To make men worse by making my sin known?
Or sin seem less, the sinner seeming great?
Alas for Arthur's greatest knight, a man
Not after Arthur's heart! I needs must break
These bonds that so defame me: not without 1410
She wills it: would I, if she will'd it? nay,
Who knows? but if I would not, then may God,
I pray him, send a sudden Angel down
To seize me by the hair and bear me far,
And fling me deep in that forgotten mere, 1415
Among the tumbled fragments of the hills."

So groaned Sir Lancelot in remorseful pain,
Not knowing he should die a holy man.

THE HOLY GRAIL

From noiseful arms, and acts of prowess done
In tournament or tilt, Sir Percivale,
Whom Arthur and his knighthood call'd The Pure,
Had pass'd into the silent life of prayer,
Praise, fast, and alms; and leaving for the cowl   5
The helmet in an abbey far away
From Camelot, there, and not long after, died.

And one, a fellow-monk among the rest,
Ambrosius, loved him much beyond the rest,
And honor'd him, and wrought into his heart   10
A way by love that waken'd love within,
To answer that which came; and as they sat
Beneath a world-old yew-tree, darkening half
The cloisters, on a gustful April morn
That puff'd the swaying branches into smoke   15
Above them, ere the summer when he died,
The monk Ambrosius question'd Percivale:

"O brother, I have seen this yew-tree smoke,
Spring after spring, for half a hundred years:
For never have I known the world without,   20
Nor ever stray'd beyond the pale: but thee,
When first thou camest — such a courtesy
Spake thro' the limbs and in the voice — I knew
For one of those who eat in Arthur's hall;
For good ye are and bad, and like to coins,   25
Some true, some light, but every one of you
Stamp'd with the image of the King; and now
Tell me, what drove thee from the Table Round,
My brother? was it earthly passion crost?"

"Nay," said the knight; "for no such passion mine
But the sweet vision of the Holy Grail   31
Drove me from all vainglories, rivalries,
And earthly heats that spring and sparkle out
Among us in the jousts, while women watch
Who wins, who falls; and waste the spiritual strength
Within us, better offer'd up to Heaven."   36

To whom the monk: "The Holy Grail! — I trust
We are green in Heaven's eyes; but here too much
We moulder — as to things without I mean —
Yet one of your own knights, a guest of ours,   40
Told us of this in our refectory,
But spake with such a sadness and so low
We heard not half of what he said. What is it?
The phantom of a cup that comes and goes?"

"Nay, monk! what phantom?" answer'd Perci-
     vale.   45
"The cup, the cup itself, from which our Lord
Drank at the last sad supper with his own.
This, from the blessed land of Aromat —
After the day of darkness, when the dead
Went wandering o'er Moriah — the good saint   50
Arimathæan Joseph, journeying brought
To Glastonbury, where the winter thorn
Blossoms at Christmas, mindful of our Lord.
And there awhile it bode; and if a man
Could touch or see it, he was heal'd at once,   55
By faith, of all his ills. But then the times
Grew to such evil that the holy cup
Was caught away to Heaven, and disappear'd."

To whom the monk: "From our old books I know

That Joseph came of old to Glastonbury,   60
And there the heathen Prince, Arviragus,
Gave him an isle of marsh whereon to build;
And there he built with wattles from the marsh
A little lonely church in days of yore,
For so they say, these books of ours, but seem   65
Mute of this miracle, far as I have read.
But who first saw the holy thing to-day?"

"A woman," answer'd Percivale, "a nun,
And one no further off in blood from me
Than sister; and if ever holy maid   70
With knees of adoration wore the stone,
A holy maid; tho' never maiden glow'd,
But that was in her earlier maidenhood,
With such a fervent flame of human love,
Which being rudely blunted, glanced and shot   75
Only to holy things; to prayer and praise
She gave herself, to fast and alms. And yet,
Nun as she was, the scandal of the Court,
Sin against Arthur and the Table Round,
And the strange sound of an adulterous race,   80
Across the iron grating of her cell
Beat, and she pray'd and fasted all the more.

"And he to whom she told her sins, or what
Her all but utter whiteness held for sin,
A man wellnigh a hundred winters old,   85
Spake often with her of the Holy Grail,
A legend handed down thro' five or six,
And each of these a hundred winters old,
From our Lord's time. And when King Arthur made
His Table Round, and all men's hearts became   90
Clean for a season, surely he had thought

That now the Holy Grail would come again,
But sin broke out. Ah, Christ, that it would come,
And heal the world of all their wickedness!
'O Father!' ask'd the maiden, 'might it come   95
To me by prayer and fasting?' 'Nay,' said he,
'I know not, for thy heart is pure as snow.'
And so she pray'd and fasted, till the sun
Shone, and the wind blew, thro' her, and I thought
She might have risen and floated when I saw her. 100

   "For on a day she sent to speak with me.
And when she came to speak, behold her eyes
Beyond my knowing of them, beautiful,
Beyond all knowing of them, wonderful,
Beautiful in the light of holiness.   105
And 'O my brother Percivale,' she said,
'Sweet brother, I have seen the Holy Grail:
For, waked at dead of night, I heard a sound
As of a silver horn from o'er the hills
Blown, and I thought, "It is not Arthur's use   110
To hunt by moonlight"; and the slender sound
As from a distance beyond distance grew
Coming upon me — O never harp nor horn,
Nor aught we blow with breath, or touch with hand,
Was like that music as it came; and then   115
Stream'd thro' my cell a cold and silver beam,
And down the long beam stole the Holy Grail,
Rose-red with beatings in it, as if alive,
Till all the white walls of my cell were dyed
With rosy colors leaping on the wall;   120
And then the music faded, and the Grail
Past, and the beam decay'd, and from the walls
The rosy quiverings died into the night.
So now the Holy Thing is here again

Among us, brother, fast thou too and pray,   125
And tell thy brother knights to fast and pray,
That so perchance the vision may be seen
By thee and those, and all the world be heal'd.'

"Then leaving the pale nun, I spake of this
To all men; and myself fasted and pray'd   130
Always, and many among us many a week
Fasted and pray'd even to the uttermost,
Expectant of the wonder that would be.

"And one there was among us, ever moved
Among us in white armor, Galahad.   135
'God make thee good as thou art beautiful,'
Said Arthur, when he dubb'd him knight; and none,
In so young youth, was ever made a knight
Till Galahad; and this Galahad, when he heard
My sister's vision, fill'd me with amaze;   140
His eyes became so like her own, they seem'd
Hers, and himself her brother more than I.

"Sister or brother none had he; but some
Call'd him a son of Lancelot, and some said
Begotten by enchantment — chatterers they,   145
Like birds of passage piping up and down,
That gape for flies — we know not whence they come;
For when was Lancelot wanderingly lewd?

"But she, the wan sweet maiden, shore away
Clean from her forehead all that wealth of hair   150
Which made a silken mat-work for her feet;
And out of this she plaited broad and long
A strong sword-belt, and wove with silver thread
And crimson in the belt a strange device,

A crimson grail within a silver beam; 155
And saw the bright boy-knight, and bound it on him,
Saying, 'My knight, my love, my knight of heaven,
O thou, my love, whose love is one with mine,
I, maiden, round thee, maiden, bind my belt.
Go forth, for thou shalt see what I have seen, 160
And break thro' all, till one will crown thee king
Far in the spiritual city': and as she spake
She sent her deathless passion in her eyes
Thro' him, and made him hers, and laid her mind
On him, and he believed in her belief. 165

"Then came a year of miracle: O brother,
In our great hall there stood a vacant chair,
Fashion'd by Merlin ere he past away,
And carven with strange figures; and in and out
The figures, like a serpent, ran a scroll 170
Of letters in a tongue no man could read.
And Merlin call'd it 'The Siege perilous.'
Perilous for good and ill; 'for there,' he said,
'No man could sit but he should lose himself.'
And once by misadventure Merlin sat 175
In his own chair, and so was lost; but he,
Galahad, when he heard of Merlin's doom,
Cried, 'If I lose myself, I save myself!'

"Then on a summer night it came to pass,
While the great banquet lay along the hall, 180
That Galahad would sit down in Merlin's chair.

"And all at once, as there we sat, we heard
A cracking and a riving of the roofs,
And rending, and a blast, and overhead
Thunder, and in the thunder was a cry. 185

And in the blast there smote along the hall
A beam of light seven times more clear than day:
And down the long beam stole the Holy Grail
All over cover'd with a luminous cloud,
And none might see who bare it, and it past.   190
But every knight beheld his fellow's face
As in a glory, and all the knights arose
And staring each at other like dumb men
Stood, till I found a voice and sware a vow.

"I sware a vow before them all, that I,   195
Because I had not seen the Grail, would ride
A twelvemonth and a day in quest of it,
Until I found and saw it, as the nun
My sister saw it; and Galahad sware the vow,
And good Sir Bors, our Lancelot's cousin, sware, 200
And Lancelot sware, and many among the knights,
And Gawain sware, and louder than the rest."

Then spake the monk Ambrosius, asking him,
"What said the King? Did Arthur take the vow?"

"Nay, for my lord," said Percivale, "the King, 205
Was not in hall: for early that same day,
Scaped thro' a cavern from a bandit hold,
An outraged maiden sprang into the hall
Crying on help: for all her shining hair
Was smear'd with earth, and either milky arm   210
Red-rent with hooks of bramble, and all she wore
Torn as a sail that leaves the rope is torn
In tempest: so the King arose and went
To smoke the scandalous hive of those wild bees
That made such honey in his realm. Howbeit   215
Some little of this marvel he too saw,

Returning o'er the plain that then began
To darken under Camelot; whence the King
Look'd up, calling aloud, 'Lo, there! the roofs
Of our great hall are roll'd in thunder-smoke!   220
Pray Heaven, they be not smitten by the bolt.'
For dear to Arthur was that hall of ours,
As having there so oft with all his knights
Feasted, and as the stateliest under heaven.

    "O brother, had you known our mighty hall,   225
Which Merlin built for Arthur long ago!
For all the sacred mount of Camelot,
And all the dim rich city, roof by roof,
Tower after tower, spire beyond spire,
By grove, and garden-lawn, and rushing brook,   230
Climbs to the mighty hall that Merlin built.
And four great zones of sculpture, set betwixt
With many a mystic symbol, gird the hall:
And in the lowest beasts are slaying men,
And in the second men are slaying beasts,   235
And on the third are warriors, perfect men,
And on the fourth are men with growing wings,
And over all one statue in the mould
Of Arthur, made by Merlin, with a crown,
And peak'd wings pointed to the Northern Star.   240
And eastward fronts the statue, and the crown
And both the wings are made of gold, and flame
At sunrise till the people in far fields,
Wasted so often by the heathen hordes,
Behold it, crying, 'We have still a King.'   245

    "And, brother, had you known our hall within,
Broader and higher than any in all the lands!
Where twelve great windows blazon Arthur's wars,

And all the light that falls upon the board
Streams thro' the twelve great battles of our King. 250
Nay, one there is, and at the eastern end,
Wealthy with wandering lines of mount and mere,
Where Arthur finds the brand Excalibur.
And also one to the west, and counter to it,
And blank: and who shall blazon it? when and
    how? —   255
O there, perchance, when all our wars are done,
The brand Excalibur will be cast away.

"So to this hall full quickly rode the King,
In horror lest the work by Merlin wrought,
Dreamlike, should on the sudden vanish, wrapt   260
In unremorseful folds of rolling fire.
And in he rode, and up I glanced, and saw
The golden dragon sparkling over all:
And many of those who burnt the hold, their arms
Hack'd, and their foreheads grimed with smoke, and
    sear'd,   265
Follow'd, and in among bright faces, ours,
Full of the vision, prest: and then the King
Spake to me, being nearest, 'Percivale,'
(Because the hall was all in tumult — some
Vowing, and some protesting), 'what is this?'   270

"O brother, when I told him what had chanced,
My sister's vision, and the rest, his face
Darken'd, as I have seen it more than once,
When some brave deed seem'd to be done in vain,
Darken; and 'Woe is me, my knights,' he cried,   275
'Had I been here, ye had not sworn the vow.'
Bold was mine answer, 'Had thyself been here,

My King, thou wouldst have sworn.' 'Yea, yea,' said
    he,
'Art thou so bold and hast not seen the Grail?'

    "'Nay, lord, I heard the sound, I saw the light, 280
But since I did not see the Holy Thing,
I sware a vow to follow it till I saw.'

    "Then when he ask'd us, knight by knight, if any
Had seen it, all their answers were as one:
'Nay, lord, and therefore have we sworn our vows.' 285

    "'Lo now,' said Arthur, 'have ye seen a cloud?
What go ye into the wilderness to see?'

    "Then Galahad on the sudden, and in a voice
Shrilling along the hall to Arthur, call'd,
'But I, Sir Arthur, saw the Holy Grail,   290
I saw the Holy Grail and heard a cry —
"O Galahad, and O Galahad, follow me."'

    "'Ah, Galahad, Galahad,' said the King, 'for such
As thou art is the vision, not for these.
Thy holy nun and thou have seen a sign —   295
Holier is none, my Percivale, than she —
A sign to maim this Order which I made.
But ye, that follow but the leader's bell'
(Brother, the King was hard upon his knights)
'Taliessin is our fullest throat of song,   300
And one hath sung and all the dumb will sing.
Lancelot is Lancelot, and hath overborne
Five knights at once, and every younger knight,
Unproven, holds himself as Lancelot,
Till overborne by one, he learns — and ye,   305

What are ye? Galahads? — no, nor Percivales'
(For thus it pleased the King to range me close
After Sir Galahad); 'nay,' said he, 'but men
With strength and will to right the wrong'd, of power
To lay the sudden heads of violence flat,   310
Knights that in twelve great battles splash'd and
    dyed
The strong White Horse in his own heathen blood —
But one hath seen, and all the blind will see.
Go, since your vows are sacred, being made:
Yet — for ye know the cries of all my realm   315
Pass thro' this hall — how often, O my knights,
Your places being vacant at my side,
This chance of noble deeds will come and go
Unchallenged, while ye follow wandering fires
Lost in the quagmire! Many of you, yea most,   320
Return no more: ye think I show myself
Too dark a prophet: come now, let us meet
The morrow morn once more in one full field
Of gracious pastime, that once more the King,
Before ye leave him for this Quest, may count   325
The yet-unbroken strength of all his knights,
Rejoicing in that Order which he made.'

"So when the sun broke next from under ground,
All the great table of our Arthur closed
And clash'd in such a tourney and so full,   330
So many lances broken — never yet
Had Camelot seen the like, since Arthur came,
And I myself and Galahad, for a strength
Was in us from the vision, overthrew
So many knights that all the people cried,   335
And almost burst the barriers in their heat,
Shouting, 'Sir Galahad and Sir Percivale!'

"But when the next day brake from under ground —
O brother, had you known our Camelot,
Built by old kings, age after age, so old   340
The King himself had fears that it would fall,
So strange, and rich, and dim; for where the roofs
Totter'd toward each other in the sky,
Met foreheads all along the street of those
Who watch'd us pass; and lower, and where the long
Rich galleries, lady-laden, weigh'd the necks   346
Of dragons clinging to the crazy walls,
Thicker than drops from thunder, showers of flowers
Fell as we past; and men and boys astride
On wyvern, lion, dragon, griffin, swan,   350
At all the corners, named us each by name,
Calling 'God speed!' but in the ways below
The knights and ladies wept, and rich and poor
Wept, and the King himself could hardly speak
For grief, and all in middle street the Queen,   355
Who rode by Lancelot, wail'd and shriek'd aloud,
'This madness has come on us for our sins.'
So to the Gate of the three Queens we came,
Where Arthur's wars are render'd mystically,
And thence departed every one his way.   360

"And I was lifted up in heart, and thought
Of all my late-shown prowess in the lists,
How my strong lance had beaten down the knights,
So many and famous names; and never yet
Had heaven appear'd so blue, nor earth so green, 365
For all my blood danced in me, and I knew
That I should light upon the Holy Grail.

"Thereafter, the dark warning of our King,
That most of us would follow wandering fires,

Came like a driving gloom across my mind.   370
Then every evil word I had spoken once,
And every evil thought I had thought of old,
And every evil deed I ever did,
Awoke and cried, 'This Quest is not for thee.'
And lifting up mine eyes, I found myself   375
Alone, and in a land of sand and thorns,
And I was thirsty even unto death;
And I, too, cried, 'This Quest is not for thee.'

"And on I rode, and when I thought my thirst
Would slay me, saw deep lawns, and then a brook, 380
With one sharp rapid, where the crisping white
Play'd ever back upon the sloping wave,
And took both ear and eye; and o'er the brook
Were apple-trees, and apples by the brook
Fallen, and on the lawns. 'I will rest here,'   385
I said, 'I am not worthy of the Quest';
But even while I drank the brook, and ate
The goodly apples, all these things at once
Fell into dust, and I was left alone,
And thirsting, in a land of sand and thorns.   390

"And then behold a woman at a door
Spinning; and fair the house whereby she sat,
And kind the woman's eyes and innocent,
And all her bearing gracious; and she rose
Opening her arms to meet me, as who should say, 395
'Rest here'; but when I touch'd her, lo! she, too,
Fell into dust and nothing, and the house
Became no better than a broken shed.
And in it a dead babe; and also this
Fell into dust, and I was left alone.   400

"And on I rode, and greater was my thirst.
Then flash'd a yellow gleam across the world,
And where it smote the plowshare in the field,
The plowman left his plowing, and fell down
Before it; where it glitter'd on her pail,   405
The milkmaid left her milking, and fell down
Before it, and I knew not why, but thought
'The sun is rising,' tho' the sun had risen.
Then was I ware of one that on me moved
In golden armor with a crown of gold   410
About a casque all jewels; and his horse
In golden armor jewell'd everywhere:
And on the splendor came, flashing me blind;
And seem'd to me the Lord of all the world,
Being so huge. But when I thought he meant   415
To crush me, moving on me, lo! he, too,
Open'd his arms to embrace me as he came,
And up I went and touch'd him, and he, too,
Fell into dust, and I was left alone
And wearying in a land of sand and thorns.   420

"And I rode on and found a mighty hill,
And on the top, a city wall'd: the spires
Prick'd with incredible pinnacles into heaven.
And by the gateway stirr'd a crowd; and these
Cried to me climbing, 'Welcome, Percivale!   425
Thou mightiest and thou purest among men!'
And glad was I and clomb, but found at top
No man, nor any voice. And thence I past
Far thro' a ruinous city, and I saw
That man had once dwelt there; but there I found   430
Only one man of an exceeding age.
'Where is that goodly company,' said I,
'That so cried out upon me?' and he had

Scarce any voice to answer, and yet gasp'd,
'Whence and what art thou?' and even as he spoke 435
Fell into dust, and disappear'd, and I
Was left alone once more, and cried in grief,
'Lo, if I find the Holy Grail itself
And touch it, it will crumble into dust.'

"And thence I dropt into a lowly vale,   440
Low as the hill was high, and where the vale
Was lowest, found a chapel, and thereby
A holy hermit in a hermitage,
To whom I told my phantoms, and he said:

"'O son, thou hast not true humility,   445
The highest virtue, mother of them all;
For when the Lord of all things made Himself
Naked of glory for His mortal change,
"Take thou my robe," she said, "for all is thine,"
And all her form shone forth with sudden light   450
So that the angels were amazed, and she
Follow'd Him down, and like a flying star
Led on the gray-hair'd wisdom of the east;
But her thou hast not known: for what is this
Thou thoughtest of thy prowess and thy sins?   455
Thou hast not lost thyself to save thyself
As Galahad.' When the hermit made an end,
In silver armor suddenly Galahad shone
Before us, and against the chapel door
Laid lance, and enter'd, and we knelt in prayer.   460
And there the hermit slaked my burning thirst,
And at the sacring of the mass I saw
The holy elements alone; but he,
'Saw ye no more? I, Galahad, saw the Grail,
The Holy Grail, descend upon the shrine: 465

I saw the fiery face as of a child
That smote itself into the bread, and went;
And hither am I come; and never yet
Hath what thy sister taught me first to see,
This Holy Thing, fail'd from my side, nor come   470
Cover'd, but moving with me night and day,
Fainter by day, but always in the night
Blood-red, and sliding down the blacken'd marsh
Blood-red, and on the naked mountain top
Blood-red, and in the sleeping mere below   475
Blood-red. And in the strength of this I rode,
Shattering all evil customs everywhere,
And past thro' Pagan realms, and made them mine,
And clash'd with Pagan hordes, and bore them down,
And broke thro' all, and in the strength of this   480
Come victor. But my time is hard at hand,
And hence I go; and one will crown me king
Far in the spiritual city; and come thou, too,
For thou shalt see the vision when I go.'

"While thus he spake, his eye, dwelling on mine,   485
Drew me, with power upon me, till I grew
One with him, to believe as he believed.
Then, when the day began to wane, we went.

"There rose a hill that none but man could climb,
Scarr'd with a hundred wintry water-courses —   490
Storm at the top, and when we gain'd it, storm
Round us and death; for every moment glanced
His silver arms and gloom'd: so quick and thick
The lightnings here and there to left and right
Struck, till the dry old trunks about us, dead,   495
Yea, rotten with a hundred years of death,
Sprang into fire: and at the base we found

On either hand, as far as eye could see,
A great black swamp and of an evil smell,
Part black, part whiten'd with the bones of men, 500
Not to be crost, save that some ancient king
Had built a way, where, link'd with many a bridge,
A thousand piers ran into the great Sea.
And Galahad fled along them bridge by bridge,
And every bridge as quickly as he crost 505
Sprang into fire and vanish'd, tho' I yearn'd
To follow; and thrice above him all the heavens
Open'd and blazed with thunder such as seem'd
Shoutings of all the sons of God: and first
At once I saw him far on the great Sea, 510
In silver-shining armor starry-clear;
And o'er his head the Holy Vessel hung
Clothed in white samite or a luminous cloud.
And with exceeding swiftness ran the boat,
If boat it were — I saw not whence it came. 515
And when the heavens open'd and blazed again
Roaring, I saw him like a silver star —
And had he set the sail, or had the boat
Become a living creature clad with wings?
And o'er his head the Holy Vessel hung 520
Redder than any rose, a joy to me,
For now I knew the veil had been withdrawn.
Then in a moment when they blazed again
Opening, I saw the least of little stars
Down on the waste, and straight beyond the star 525
I saw the spiritual city and all her spires
And gateways in a glory like one pearl —
No larger, tho' the goal of all the saints —
Strike from the sea; and from the star there shot
A rose-red sparkle to the city, and there 530
Dwelt, and I know it was the Holy Grail,

Which never eyes on earth again shall see.
Then fell the floods of heaven drowning the deep
And how my feet recrost the deathful ridge
No memory in me lives; but that I touch'd   535
The chapel-doors at dawn I know; and thence
Taking my war-horse from the holy man,
Glad that no phantom vext me more, return'd
To whence I came, the gate of Arthur's wars."

  "O brother," ask'd Ambrosius, — "for in sooth
These ancient books — and they would win thee —
     teem,   541
Only I find not there this Holy Grail,
With miracles and marvels like to these,
Not all unlike; which oftentime I read,
Who read but on my breviary with ease,   545
Till my head swims; and then go forth and pass
Down to the little thorpe that lies so close,
And almost plaster'd like a martin's nest
To these old walls — and mingle with our folk;
And knowing every honest face of theirs   550
As well as ever shepherd knew his sheep,
And every homely secret in their hearts,
Delight myself with gossip and old wives,
And ills and aches, and teethings, lyings-in,
And mirthful sayings, children of the place,   555
That have no meaning half a league away:
Or lulling random squabbles when they rise,
Chafferings and chatterings at the market-cross,
Rejoice, small man, in this small world of mine,
Yea, even in their hens and in their eggs —   560
O brother, saving this Sir Galahad,
Came ye on none but phantoms in your quest,
No man, no woman?"

Then Sir Percivale:
"All men, to one so bound by such a vow,
And women were as phantoms. O, my brother,   565
Why wilt thou shame me to confess to thee
How far I falter'd from my quest and vow?
For after I had lain so many nights,
A bedmate of the snail and eft and snake,
In grass and burdock, I was changed to wan   570
And meagre, and the vision had not come;
And then I chanced upon a goodly town
With one great dwelling in the middle of it;
Thither I made, and there was I disarm'd
By maidens each as fair as any flower: 575
But when they led me into hall, behold,
The Princess of that castle was the one,
Brother, and that one only, who had ever
Made my heart leap; for when I moved of old
A slender page about her father's hall,   580
And she a slender maiden, all my heart
Went after her with longing: yet we twain
Had never kiss'd a kiss, or vow'd a vow.
And now I came upon her once again,
And one had wedded her, and he was dead,   585
And all his land and wealth and state were hers.
And while I tarried, every day she set
A banquet richer than the day before
By me; for all her longing and her will
Was toward me as of old; till one fair morn,   590
I walking to and fro beside a stream
That flash'd across her orchard underneath
Her castle-walls, she stole upon my walk,
And calling me the greatest of all knights,
Embraced me, and so kiss'd me the first time,   595
And gave herself and all her wealth to me.

Then I remember'd Arthur's warning word,
That most of us would follow wandering fires,
And the Quest faded in my heart. Anon,
The heads of all her people drew to me,   600
With supplication both of knees and tongue:
'We have heard of thee: thou art our greatest knight,
Our Lady says it, and we well believe:
Wed thou our Lady, and rule over us,
And thou shalt be as Arthur in our land.'   605
O me, my brother! but one night my vow
Burnt me within, so that I rose and fled,
But wail'd and wept, and hated mine own self,
And ev'n the Holy Quest, and all but her;
Then after I was join'd with Galahad   610
Cared not for her, nor anything upon earth."

    Then said the monk, "Poor men, when yule is
        cold,
Must be content to sit by little fires.
And this am I, so that ye care for me
Ever so little; yea, and blest be Heaven   615
That brought thee here to this poor house of ours
Where all the brethren are so hard, to warm
My cold heart with a friend: but O the pity
To find thine own first love once more — to hold,
Hold her a wealthy bride within thine arms,   620
Or all but hold, and then — cast her aside,
Foregoing all her sweetness, like a weed.
For we that want the warmth of double life,
We that are plagued with dreams of something sweet
Beyond all sweetness in a life so rich, —   625
Ah, blessed Lord, I speak too earthlywise,
Seeing I never stray'd beyond the cell,
But live like an old badger in his earth,

With earth about him everywhere, despite
All fast and penance. Saw ye none beside,   630
None of your knights?"

                       "Yea so," said Percivale:
"One night my pathway swerving east, I saw
The pelican on the casque of our Sir Bors
All in the middle of the rising moon:
And toward him spurr'd, and hail'd him, and he me,
And each made joy of either; then he ask'd,   636
'Where is he? hast thou seen him — Lancelot? —
    Once,'
Said good Sir Bors, 'he dash'd across me — mad,
And maddening what he rode: and when I cried,
"Ridest thou then so hotly on a quest   640
So holy," Lancelot shouted, "Stay me not!
I have been the sluggard, and I ride apace,
For now there is a lion in the way."
So vanish'd.'

            "Then Sir Bors had ridden on
Softly, and sorrowing for our Lancelot,   645
Because his former madness, once the talk
And scandal of our table, had return'd;
For Lancelot's kith and kin so worship him
That ill to him is ill to them; to Bors
Beyond the rest: he well had been content   650
Not to have seen, so Lancelot might have seen,
The Holy Cup of healing; and, indeed,
Being so clouded with his grief and love,
Small heart was his after the Holy Quest:
If God would send the vision, well: if not,   655
The Quest and he were in the hands of Heaven.

"And then, with small adventure met, Sir Bors
Rode to the lonest tract of all the realm,
And found a people there among their crags,
Our race and blood, a remnant that were left   660
Paynim amid their circles, and the stones
They pitch up straight to heaven: and their wise men
Were strong in that old magic which can trace
The wandering of the stars, and scoff'd at him
And this high Quest as at a simple thing: 665
Told him he follow'd — almost Arthur's words —
A mocking fire: 'what other fire than he,
Whereby the blood beats, and the blossom blows,
And the sea rolls, and all the world is warm'd?'
And when his answer chafed them, the rough crowd,
Hearing he had a difference with their priests,   671
Seized him, and bound and plunged him into a cell
Of great piled stones; and lying bounden there
In darkness thro' innumerable hours
He heard the hollow-ringing heavens sweep   675
Over him till by miracle — what else? —
Heavy as it was, a great stone slipt and fell,
Such as no wind could move: and thro' the gap
Glimmer'd the streaming scud: then came a night
Still as the day was loud; and thro' the gap   680
The seven clear stars of Arthur's Table Round —
For, brother, so one night, because they roll
Thro' such a round in heaven, we named the stars,
Rejoicing in ourselves and in our King —
And these, like bright eyes of familiar friends,   685
In on him shone: 'And then to me, to me,'
Said good Sir Bors, 'beyond all hopes of mine,
Who scarce had pray'd or ask'd it for myself —
Across the seven clear stars — O grace to me —
In color like the fingers of a hand   690

Before a burning taper, the sweet Grail
Glided and past, and close upon it peal'd
A sharp quick thunder.' Afterwards, a maid,
Who kept our holy faith among her kin
In secret, entering, loosed and let him go."   695

To whom the monk: "And I remember now
That pelican on the casque: Sir Bors it was
Who spake so low and sadly at our board;
And mighty reverent at our grace was he:
A square-set man and honest; and his eyes,   700
An out-door sign of all the warmth within,
Smiled with his lips — a smile beneath a cloud,
But heaven had meant it for a sunny one:
Ay, ay, Sir Bors, who else? But when ye reach'd
The city, found ye all your knights return'd,   705
Or was there sooth in Arthur's prophecy,
Tell me, and what said each, and what the King?"

Then answer'd Percivale: "And that can I,
Brother, and truly; since the living words
Of so great men as Lancelot and our King   710
Pass not from door to door and out again,
But sit within the house. O, when we reach'd
The city, our horses stumbling as they trode
On heaps of ruin, hornless unicorns,
Crack'd basilisks, and splinter'd cockatrices,   715
And shatter'd talbots, which had left the stones
Raw, that they fell from, brought us to the hall.

"And there sat Arthur on the daïs-throne,
And those that had gone out upon the Quest,
Wasted and worn, and but a tithe of them,   720
And those that had not, stood before the King,

Who, when he saw me, rose, and bade me hail,
Saying, 'A welfare in thine eye reproves
Our fear of some disastrous chance for thee
On hill, or plain, at sea, or flooding ford.   725
So fierce a gale made havoc here of late
Among the strange devices of our kings;
Yea, shook this newer, stronger hall of ours,
And from the statue Merlin moulded for us
Half-wrench'd a golden wing; but now — the Quest,
This vision — hast thou seen the Holy Cup,   731
That Joseph brought of old to Glastonbury?'

    "So when I told him all thyself hast heard,
Ambrosius, and my fresh but fixt resolve
To pass away into the quiet life,   735
He answer'd not, but, sharply turning, ask'd
Of Gawain, 'Gawain, was this Quest for thee?'

    "'Nay, lord,' said Gawain, 'not for such as I.
Therefore I communed with a saintly man,
Who made me sure the Quest was not for me;   740
For I was much awearied of the Quest:
But found a silk pavilion in a field,
And merry maidens in it; and then this gale
Tore my pavilion from the tenting-pin,
And blew my merry maidens all about   745
With all discomfort; yea, and but for this,
My twelvemonth and a day were pleasant to me.'

    "He ceased; and Arthur turn'd to whom at first
He saw not, for Sir Bors, on entering, push'd
Athwart the throng to Lancelot, caught his hand,   750
Held it, and there, half-hidden by him, stood,
Until the King espied him, saying to him,

'Hail, Bors! if ever loyal man and true
Could see it, thou hast seen the Grail'; and Bors,
'Ask me not, for I may not speak of it: 755
I saw it'; and the tears were in his eyes.

"Then there remain'd but Lancelot, for the rest
Spake but of sundry perils in the storm;
Perhaps, like him of Cana in Holy Writ,
Our Arthur kept his best until the last;   760
'Thou, too, my Lancelot,' ask'd the King, 'my friend,
Our mightiest, hath this Quest avail'd for thee?'

"'Our mightiest!' answer'd Lancelot, with a groan;
'O King!'— and when he paused, methought I spied
A dying fire of madness in his eyes —   765
'O King, my friend, if friend of thine I be,
Happier are those that welter in their sin,
Swine in the mud, that cannot see for slime,
Slime of the ditch: but in me lived a sin
So strange, of such a kind, that all of pure,   770
Noble, and knightly in me twined and clung
Round that one sin, until the wholesome flower
And poisonous grew together, each as each,
Not to be pluck'd asunder; and when thy knights
Sware, I sware with them only in the hope   775
That could I touch or see the Holy Grail
They might be pluck'd asunder. Then I spake
To one most holy saint, who wept and said,
That save they could be pluck'd asunder, all
My quest were but in vain; to whom I vow'd   780
That I would work according as he will'd.
And forth I went, and while I yearn'd and strove
To tear the twain asunder in my heart,
My madness came upon me as of old,

And whipt me into waste fields far away; 785
There was I beaten down by little men,
Mean knights, to whom the moving of my sword
And shadow of my spear had been enow
To scare them from me once; and then I came
All in my folly to the naked shore, 790
Wide flats, where nothing but coarse grasses grew;
But such a blast, my King, began to blow,
So loud a blast along the shore and sea,
Ye could not hear the waters for the blast,
Tho' heapt in mounds and ridges all the sea 795
Drove like a cataract, and all the sand
Swept like a river, and the clouded heavens
Were shaken with the motion and the sound.
And blackening in the sea-foam sway'd a boat,
Half-swallow'd in it, anchor'd with a chain; 800
And in my madness to myself I said,
"I will embark and I will lose myself,
And in the great sea wash away my sin."
I burst the chain, I sprang into the boat.
Seven days I drove along the dreary deep, 805
And with me drove the moon and all the stars;
And the wind fell, and on the seventh night
I heard the shingle grinding in the surge,
And felt the boat shock earth, and looking up,
Behold, the enchanted towers of Carbonek, 810
A castle like a rock upon a rock,
With chasm-like portals open to the sea,
And steps that met the breaker! there was none
Stood near it but a lion on each side
That kept the entry, and the moon was full. 815
Then from the boat I leapt, and up the stairs.
There drew my sword. With sudden flaring manes
Those two great beasts rose upright like a man,

Each gript a shoulder, and I stood between;
And, when I would have smitten them, heard a voice,
"Doubt not, go forward; if thou doubt, the beasts   821
Will tear thee piecemeal." Then with violence
The sword was dash'd from out my hand, and fell.
And up into the sounding hall I past;
But nothing in the sounding hall I saw,   825
No bench nor table, painting on the wall
Or shield of knight; only the rounded moon
Thro' the tall oriel on the rolling sea.
But always in the quiet house I heard,
Clear as a lark, high o'er me as a lark,   830
A sweet voice singing in the topmost tower
To the eastward: up I climb'd a thousand steps
With pain: as in a dream I seem'd to climb
For ever: at the last I reach'd a door,
A light was in the crannies, and I heard,   835
"Glory and joy and honor to our Lord
And to the Holy Vessel of the Grail."
Then in my madness I essay'd the door;
It gave; and thro' a stormy glare, a heat
As from a seventimes-heated furnace, I,   840
Blasted and burnt, and blinded as I was,
With such a fierceness that I swoon'd away —
O, yet methought I saw the Holy Grail,
All pall'd in crimson samite, and around
Great angels, awful shapes, and wings and eyes.   845
And but for all my madness and my sin,
And then my swooning, I had sworn I saw
That which I saw; but what I saw was veil'd
And cover'd; and this Quest was not for me.'

"So speaking, and here ceasing, Lancelot left   850
The hall long silent, till Sir Gawain — nay,

Brother, I need not tell thee foolish words, —
A reckless and irreverent knight was he,
Now bolden'd by the silence of his King, —
Well, I tell thee: 'O King, my liege,' he said,   855
'Hath Gawain fail'd in any quest of thine?
When have I stinted stroke in foughten field?
But as for thine, my good friend Percivale,
Thy holy nun and thou have driven men mad,
Yea, made our mightiest madder than our least.   860
But by mine eyes and by mine ears I swear,
I will be deafer than the blue-eyed cat,
And thrice as blind as any noonday owl,
To holy virgins in their ecstasies,
Henceforward.'

          "'Deafer,' said the blameless King,
'Gawain, and blinder unto holy things,   866
Hope not to make thyself by idle vows,
Being too blind to have desire to see.
But if indeed there came a sign from heaven,
Blessed are Bors, Lancelot and Percivale,   870
For these have seen according to their sight.
For every fiery prophet in old times,
And all the sacred madness of the bard,
When God made music thro' them, could but speak
His music by the framework and the chord;   875
And as ye saw it ye have spoken truth.

          "'Nay — but thou errest, Lancelot; never yet
Could all of true and noble in knight and man
Twine round one sin, whatever it might be,
With such a closeness, but apart there grew,   880
Save that he were the swine thou spakest of,
Some root of knighthood and pure nobleness;
Whereto see thou, that it may bear its flower.

"'And spake I not too truly, O my knights?
Was I too dark a prophet when I said   885
To those who went upon the Holy Quest,
That most of them would follow wandering fires.
Lost in the quagmire? — lost to me and gone,
And left me gazing at a barren board,
And a lean Order — scarce return'd a tithe —   890
And out of those to whom the vision came
My greatest hardly will believe he saw;
Another hath beheld it afar off,
And leaving human wrongs to right themselves,
Cares but to pass into the silent life.   895
And one hath had the vision face to face,
And now his chair desires him here in vain,
However they may crown him otherwhere.

"'And some among you held that if the King
Had seen the sight he would have sworn the vow: 900
Not easily, seeing that the King must guard
That which he rules, and is but as the hind
To whom a space of land is given to plow.
Who may not wander from the allotted field
Before his work be done; but, being done,   905
Let visions of the night or of the day
Come, as they will; and many a time they come,
Until this earth he walks on seems not earth,
This light that strikes his eyeball is not light,
This air that smites his forehead is not air   910
But vision — yea, his very hand and foot —
In moments when he feels he cannot die,
And knows himself no vision to himself,
Nor the high God a vision, nor that One
Who rose again: ye have seen what ye have seen.' 915

"So spake the King: I knew not all he meant."

THE PASSING OF ARTHUR

THAT story which the bold Sir Bedivere,
First made and latest left of all the knights,
Told, when the man was no more than a voice
In the white winter of his age, to those
With whom he dwelt, new faces, other minds.   5

For on their march to westward, Bedivere,
Who slowly paced among the slumbering host,
Heard in his tent the moanings of the King:

" I found Him in the shining of the stars,
I mark'd Him in the flowering of His fields,   10
But in His ways with men I find Him not.
I waged His wars, and now I pass and die.
O me! for why is all around us here
As if some lesser god had made the world,
But had not force to shape it as he would,   15
Till the High God behold it from beyond,
And enter it, and make it beautiful?
Or else as if the world were wholly fair,
But that these eyes of men are dense and dim,
And have not power to see it as it is: 20
Perchance, because we see not to the close; —
For I, being simple, thought to work His will,
And have but stricken with the sword in vain;
And all whereon I lean'd in wife and friend
Is traitor to my peace, and all my realm   25
Reels back into the beast, and is no more.
My God, thou hast forgotten me in my death:
Nay — God my Christ — I pass but shall not die."

Then, ere that last weird battle in the west,
There came on Arthur sleeping, Gawain kill'd   30
In Lancelot's war, the ghost of Gawain blown
Along a wandering wind, and past his ear
Went shrilling, " Hollow, hollow all delight!
Hail, King! to-morrow thou shalt pass away.
Farewell! there is an isle of rest for thee.   35
And I am blown along a wandering wind,
And hollow, hollow, hollow all delight."
And fainter onward, like wild birds that change
Their season in the night and wail their way
From cloud to cloud, down the long wind the dream
Shrill'd; but in going mingled with dim cries   41
Far in the moonlit haze among the hills,
As of some lonely city sack'd by night,
When all is lost, and wife and child with wail
Pass to new lords; and Arthur woke and call'd,   45
" Who spake? A dream. O light upon the wind,
Thine, Gawain, was the voice — are these dim cries
Thine? or doth all that haunts the waste and wild
Mourn, knowing it will go along with me?"

This heard the bold Sir Bedivere and spake: 50
" O me, my King, let pass whatever will,
Elves, and the harmless glamour of the field;
But in their stead thy name and glory cling
To all high places like a golden cloud
For ever: but as yet thou shalt not pass.   55
Light was Gawain in life, and light in death
Is Gawain, for the ghost is as the man;
And care not thou for dreams from him, but rise —
I hear the steps of Modred in the west,
And with him many of thy people, and knights   60
Once thine, whom thou hast loved, but grosser grown

Peter Vischer

KING ARTHUR

Than heathen, spitting at their vows and thee.
Right well in heart they know thee for the King.
Arise, go forth and conquer as of old."

Then spake King Arthur to Sir Bedivere: 65
"Far other is this battle in the west
Whereto we move, than when we strove in youth,
And brake the petty kings, and fought with Rome,
Or thrust the heathen from the Roman wall,
And shook him thro' the north. Ill doom is mine   70
To war against my people and my knights.
The king who fights his people fights himself.
And they my knights, who loved me once, the stroke
That strikes them dead is as my death to me.
Yet let us hence, and find or feel a way   75
Thro' this blind haze, which ever since I saw
One lying in the dust at Almesbury,
Hath folded in the passes of the world."

Then rose the King and moved his host by night,
And ever push'd Sir Modred, league by league,   80
Back to the sunset bound of Lyonnesse —
A land of old upheaven from the abyss
By fire, to sink into the abyss again;
Where fragments of forgotten peoples dwelt,
And the long mountains ended in a coast   85
Of ever-shifting sand, and far away
The phantom circle of a moaning sea.
There the pursuer could pursue no more,
And he that fled no further fly the King;
And there, that day when the great light of heaven   90
Burn'd at his lowest in the rolling year,
On the waste sand by the waste sea they closed.
Nor ever yet had Arthur fought a fight

Like this last, dim, weird battle of the west.
A deathwhite mist slept over sand and sea :   95
Whereof the chill, to him who breathed it, drew
Down with his blood, till all his heart was cold
With formless fear; and ev'n on Arthur fell
Confusion, since he saw not whom he fought.
For friend and foe were shadows in the mist,   100
And friend slew friend not knowing whom he slew;
And some had visions out of golden youth,
And some beheld the faces of old ghosts
Look in upon the battle ; and in the mist
Was many a noble deed, many a base,   105
And chance and craft and strength in single fights,
And ever and anon with host to host
Shocks, and the splintering spear, the hard mail hewn,
Shield-breakings, and the clash of brands, the crash
Of battle-axes on shatter'd helms, and shrieks   110
After the Christ, of those who falling down
Look'd up for heaven, and only saw the mist;
And shouts of heathen and the traitor knights,
Oaths, insult, filth, and monstrous blasphemies,
Sweat, writhings, anguish, laboring of the lungs   115
In that close mist, and cryings for the light,
Moans of the dying, and voices of the dead.

Last, as by some one deathbed after wail
Of suffering, silence follows, or thro' death
Or deathlike swoon, thus over all that shore,   120
Save for some whisper of the seething seas,
A dead hush fell; but when the dolorous day
Grew drearier toward twilight falling, came
A bitter wind, clear from the North, and blew
The mist aside, and with that wind the tide   125
Rose, and the pale King glanced across the field

Of battle: but no man was moving there;
Nor any cry of Christian heard thereon,
Nor yet of heathen; only the wan wave
Brake in among dead faces, to and fro   130
Swaying the helpless hands, and up and down
Tumbling the hollow helmets of the fallen,
And shiver'd brands that once had fought with Rome,
And rolling far along the gloomy shores
The voice of days of old and days to be.   135

Then spake King Arthur to Sir Bedivere,
And whiter than the mist that all day long
Had held the field of battle was the King:

"Hearest thou this great voice that shakes the world,
And wastes the narrow realm whereon we move,   140
And beats upon the faces of the dead,
My dead, as tho' they had not died for me?—
O Bedivere, for on my heart hath fall'n
Confusion, till I know not what I am,
Nor whence I am, nor whether I be King.   145
Behold, I seem but King among the dead."

Then spake the bold Sir Bedivere: "My King,
King everywhere! and so the dead have kings,
There also will I worship thee as King.
Yet still thy life is whole, and still I live   150
Who love thee; but who hates thee, he that brought
The heathen back among us, yonder stands,
Modred, unharm'd, the traitor of thine house."

Then spake the King: "My house hath been my
        doom.
But call not thou this traitor of my house   155

Who hath but dwelt beneath one roof with me.
My house are rather they who sware my vows,
Yea, even while they brake them, own'd me King.
And well for thee, saying in my dark hour,
When all the purport of my throne hath fail'd,   160
That quick or dead thou holdest me for King.
King am I, whatsoever be their cry;
And one last act of kinghood shalt thou see
Yet, ere I pass." And uttering this the King
Made at the man: then Modred smote his liege   165
Hard on that helm which many a heathen sword
Had beaten thin; while Arthur at one blow,
Striking the last stroke with Excalibur,
Slew him, and all but slain himself, he fell.

So all day long the noise of battle roll'd   170
Among the mountains by the winter sea;
Until King Arthur's Table, man by man,
Had fall'n in Lyonnesse about their lord,
King Arthur. Then, because his wound was deep,
The bold Sir Bedivere uplifted him,   175
And bore him to a chapel nigh the field,
A broken chancel with a broken cross,
That stood on a dark strait of barren land:
On one side lay the Ocean, and on one
Lay a great water, and the moon was full.   180

Then spake King Arthur to Sir Bedivere:
" The sequel of to-day unsolders all
The goodliest fellowship of famous knights
Whereof this world holds record. Such a sleep
They sleep — the men I loved. I think that we   185
Shall never more, at any future time,
Delight our souls with talk of knightly deeds,

Walking about the gardens and the halls
Of Camelot, as in the days that were.
I perish by this people which I made, —   190
Tho' Merlin sware that I should come again
To rule once more ; but, let what will be, be,
I am so deeply smitten thro' the helm
That without help I cannot last till morn.
Thou therefore take my brand Excalibur,   19[
Which was my pride : for thou rememberest how
In those old days, one summer noon, an arm
Rose up from out the bosom of the lake,
Clothed in white samite, mystic, wonderful,
Holding the sword — and how I row'd across   200
And took it, and have worn it, like a king;
And, wheresoever I am sung or told
In aftertime, this also shall be known :
But now delay not : take Excalibur,
And fling him far into the middle mere :   205
Watch what thou seëst, and lightly bring me word."

To him replied the bold Sir Bedivere :
" It is not meet, Sir King, to leave thee thus,
Aidless, alone, and smitten thro' the helm —
A little thing may harm a wounded man ;   210
Yet I thy hest will all perform at full,
Watch what I see, and lightly bring thee word."

So saying, from the ruin'd shrine he stept,
And in the moon athwart the place of tombs,
Where lay the mighty bones of ancient men,   215
Old knights, and over them the sea-wind sang
Shrill, chill, with flakes of foam. He, stepping down
By zigzag paths, and juts of pointed rock,
Came on the shining levels of the lake.

There drew he forth the brand Excalibur,   220
And o'er him, drawing it, the winter moon,
Brightening the skirts of a long cloud, ran forth
And sparkled keen with frost against the hilt:
For all the haft twinkled with diamond sparks,
Myriads of topaz-lights, and jacinth-work   225
Of subtlest jewelry. He gazed so long
That both his eyes were dazzled as he stood,
This way and that dividing the swift mind,
In act to throw: but at the last it seem'd
Better to leave Excalibur conceal'd   230
There in the many-knotted waterflags,
That whistled stiff and dry about the marge.
So strode he back slow to the wounded King.

Then spake King Arthur to Sir Bedivere:
"Hast thou perform'd my mission which I gave?   235
What is it thou hast seen? or what hast heard?"

And answer made the bold Sir Bedivere:
"I heard the ripple washing in the reeds,
And the wild water lapping on the crag."

To whom replied King Arthur, faint and pale: 240
"Thou hast betray'd thy nature and thy name,
Not rendering true answer, as beseem'd
Thy fëalty, nor like a noble knight:
For surer sign had follow'd, either hand,
Or voice, or else a motion of the mere.   245
This is a shameful thing for men to lie.
Yet now, I charge thee, quickly go again,
As thou art lief and dear, and do the thing
I bade thee, watch, and lightly bring me word."

Then went Sir Bedivere the second time 250
Across the ridge, and paced beside the mere,
Counting the dewy pebbles, fix'd in thought;
But when he saw the wonder of the hilt,
How curiously and strangely chased, he smote
His palms together, and he cried aloud : 255

" And if indeed I cast the brand away,
Surely a precious thing, one worthy note,
Should thus be lost for ever from the earth,
Which might have pleased the eyes of many men.
What good should follow this, if this were done? 260
What harm, undone? Deep harm to disobey,
Seeing obedience is the bond of rule.
Were it well to obey then, if a king demand
An act unprofitable, against himself?
The King is sick, and knows not what he does. 265
What record, or what relic of my lord
Should be to aftertime, but empty breath
And rumors of a doubt? But were this kept,
Stored in some treasure-house of mighty kings,
Some onè might show it at a joust of arms, 270
Saying, ' King Arthur's sword, Excalibur,
Wrought by the lonely maiden of the Lake.
Nine years she wrought it, sitting in the deeps
Upon the hidden bases of the hills.'
So might some old man speak in the aftertime 275
To all the people, winning reverence.
But now much honor and much fame were lost."

So spake he, clouded with his own conceit,
And hid Excalibur the second time,
And so strode back slow to the wounded King. 280

Then spoke King Arthur, breathing heavily:
" What is it thou hast seen? or what hast heard?"

And answer made the bold Sir Bedivere:
" I heard the water lapping on the crag,
And the long ripple washing in the reeds."   285

To whom replied King Arthur, much in wrath:
" Ah, miserable and unkind, untrue,
Unknightly, traitor-hearted! Woe is me!
Authority forgets a dying king,
Laid widow'd of the power in his eye   290
That bowed the will. I see thee what thou art,
For thou, the latest-left of all my knights,
In whom should meet the offices of all,
Thou wouldst betray me for the precious hilt;
Either from lust of gold, or like a girl   295
Valuing the giddy pleasure of the eyes.
Yet, for a man may fail in duty twice,
And the third time may prosper, get thee hence:
But, if thou spare to fling Excalibur,
I will arise and slay thee with my hands."   300

Then quickly rose Sir Bedivere, and ran,
And, leaping down the ridges lightly, plunged
Among the bulrush beds, and clutch'd the sword,
And strongly wheel'd and threw it. The great brand
Made lightnings in the splendor of the moon,   305
And flashing round and round, and whirl'd in an arch,
Shot like a streamer of the northern morn,
Seen where the moving isles of winter shock
By night, with noises of the Northern Sea.
So flash'd and fell the brand Excalibur: 310
But ere he dipt the surface, rose an arm

Clothed in white samite, mystic, wonderful,
And caught him by the hilt, and brandish'd him
Three times, and drew him under in the mere.
And lightly went the other to the King.   315

Then spoke King Arthur, drawing thicker breath:
" Now see I by thine eyes that this is done.
Speak out: what is it thou hast heard, or seen ? "

And answer made the bold Sir Bedivere:
" Sir King, I closed mine eyelids, lest the gems   320
Should blind my purpose, for I never saw,
Nor shall see, here or elsewhere, till I die,
Not tho' I live three lives of mortal men,
So great a miracle as yonder hilt.
Then with both hands I flung him, wheeling him ;   325
But when I look'd again, behold an arm,
Clothed in white samite, mystic, wonderful,
That caught him by the hilt, and brandish'd him
Three times, and drew him under in the mere."

And answer made King Arthur, breathing hard:
" My end draws nigh; 't is time that I were gone,   331
Make broad thy shoulders to receive my weight,
And bear me to the margin ; yet I fear
My wound hath taken cold, and I shall die."

So saying, from the pavement he half rose,   335
Slowly, with pain, reclining on his arm,
And looking wistfully with wide blue eyes
As in a picture. Him Sir Bedivere
Remorsefully regarded thro' his tears,
And would have spoken, but he found not words ;   340
Then took with care, and kneeling on one knee,

O'er both his shoulders drew the languid hands,
And rising bore him thro' the place of tombs.

But, as he walk'd, King Arthur panted hard,
Like one that feels a nightmare on his bed   345
When all the house is mute. So sigh'd the King,
Muttering and murmuring at his ear, "Quick, quick!
I fear it is too late, and I shall die."
But the other swiftly strode from ridge to ridge,
Clothed with his breath, and looking, as he walk'd,
Larger than human on the frozen hills.   351
He heard the deep behind him, and a cry
Before. His own thought drove him like a goad.
Dry clash'd his harness in the icy caves
And barren chasms, and all to left and right   355
The bare black cliff clang'd round him, as he
     based
His feet on juts of slippery crag that rang
Sharp-smitten with the dint of armed heels —
And on a sudden, lo! the level lake,
And the long glories of the winter moon.   360

Then saw they how there hove a dusky barge,
Dark as a funeral scarf from stem to stern,
Beneath them; and descending they were ware
That all the decks were dense with stately forms,
Black-stoled, black-hooded, like a dream — by these
Three Queens with crowns of gold: and from them
     rose   366
A cry that shiver'd to the tingling stars,
And as it were one voice, an agony
Of lamentation, like a wind that shrills
All night in a waste land, where no one comes,   370
Or hath come, since the making of the world.

Then murmur'd Arthur, " Place me in the barge."
So to the barge they came. There those three Queens
Put forth their hands, and took the King, and wept.
But she, that rose the tallest of them all   375
And fairest, laid his head upon her lap,
And loosed the shatter'd casque, and chafed his hands,
And call'd him by his name, complaining loud,
And dropping bitter tears against a brow
Striped with dark blood: for all his face was white
And colorless, and like the wither'd moon   381
Smote by the fresh beam of the springing east;
And all his greaves and cuisses dash'd with drops
Of onset; and the light and lustrous curls —
That made his forehead like a rising sun   385
High from the daïs-throne — were parch'd with dust,
Or, clotted into points and hanging loose,
Mix'd with the knightly growth that fringed his
          lips.
So like a shatter'd column lay the King;
Not like that Arthur who, with lance in rest,   390
From spur to plume a star of tournament,
Shot thro' the lists at Camelot, and charged
Before the eyes of ladies and of kings.

Then loudly cried the bold Sir Bedivere :
" Ah! my Lord Arthur, whither shall I go?   395
Where shall I hide my forehead and my eyes?
For now I see the true old times are dead,
When every morning brought a noble chance,
And every chance brought out a noble knight.
Such times have been not since the light that led 400
The holy Elders with the gift of myrrh.
But now the whole Round Table is dissolved
Which was an image of the mighty world,

And I, the last, go forth companionless,
And the days darken round me, and the years,   405
Among new men, strange faces, other minds."

And slowly answer'd Arthur from the barge:
" The old order changeth, yielding place to new,
And God fulfils himself in many ways,
Lest one good custom should corrupt the world.   410
Comfort thyself : what comfort is in me ?
I have lived my life, and that which I have done
May He within himself make pure ! but thou,
If thou shouldst never see my face again,   414
Pray for my soul. More things are wrought by prayer
Than this world dreams of. Wherefore, let thy voice
Rise like a fountain for me night and day.
For what are men better than sheep or goats
That nourish a blind life within the brain,
If, knowing God, they lift not hands of prayer   420
Both for themselves and those who call them friend ?
For so the whole round earth is every way
Bound by gold chains about the feet of God.
But now farewell. I am going a long way
With these thou seëst — if indeed I go   425
(For all my mind is clouded with a doubt) —
To the island-valley of Avilion ;
Where falls not hail, or rain, or any snow,
Nor ever wind blows loudly ; but it lies
Deep-meadow'd, happy, fair with orchard lawns   430
And bowery hollows crown'd with summer sea,
Where I will heal me of my grievous wound."

So said he, and the barge with oar and sail
Moved from the brink, like some full-breasted swan
That, fluting a wild carol ere her death,   435

Ruffles her pure cold plume, and takes the flood
With swarthy webs. Long stood Sir Bedivere
Revolving many memories, till the hull
Look'd one black dot against the verge of dawn,
And on the mere the wailing died away.   440

But when that moan had past for evermore,
The stillness of the dead world's winter dawn
Amazed him, and he groan'd, "The King is gone."
And therewithal came on him the weird rhyme,
"From the great deep to the great deep he goes." 445

Whereas he slowly turn'd and slowly clomb
The last hard footstep of that iron crag;
Thence mark'd the black hull moving yet, and cried,
"He passes to be King among the dead,
And after healing of his grievous wound   450
He comes again; but — if he come no more —
O me, be yon dark Queens in yon black boat,
Who shriek'd and wail'd, the three whereat we gazed
On that high day, when, clothed with living light,
They stood before his throne in silence, friends   455
Of Arthur, who should help him at his need?"

Then from the dawn it seem'd there came, but faint
As from beyond the limit of the world,
Like the last echo born of a great cry,
Sounds, as if some fair city were one voice   460
Around a king returning from his wars.

Thereat once more he moved about, and clomb
Ev'n to the highest he could climb, and saw,
Straining his eyes beneath an arch of hand,
Or thought he saw, the speck that bare the King,   465

Down that long water opening on the deep
Somewhere far off, pass on and on, and go
From less to less and vanish into light.
And the new sun rose bringing the new year.

KING ARTHUR'S ROUND TABLE

Now in Winchester Castle.   A work of art of doubtful date, 1235-1425.

TO THE QUEEN

O LOYAL to the royal in thyself,
And loyal to thy land, as this to thee ——
Bear witness, that rememberable day,
When, pale as yet, and fever-worn, the Prince
Who scarce had pluck'd his flickering life again   5
From halfway down the shadow of the grave,
Past with thee thro' thy people and their love,
And London roll'd one tide of joy thro' all
Her trebled millions, and loud leagues of man
And welcome! witness, too, the silent cry,   10
The prayer of many a race and creed, and clime —
Thunderless lightnings striking under sea
From sunset and sunrise of all thy realm,
And that true North, whereof we lately heard
A strain to shame us "keep you to yourselves ;   15
So loyal is too costly! friends — your love
Is but a burthen : loose the bond, and go."
Is this the tone of empire? here the faith
That made us rulers? this, indeed, her voice
And meaning, whom the roar of Hougoumont   20
Left mightiest of all peoples under heaven?
What shock has fool'd her since, that she should speak
So feebly? wealthier — wealthier — hour by hour !
The voice of Britain, or a sinking land,
Some third-rate isle half-lost among her seas?   25
There rang her voice, when the full city peal'd
Thee and thy Prince ! The loyal to their crown
Are loyal to their own far sons, who love
Our ocean-empire with her boundless homes
For ever-broadening England, and her throne   30

In our vast Orient, and one isle, one isle,
That knows not her own greatness: if she knows
And dreads it we are fall'n. —— But thou, my Queen,
Not for itself, but thro' thy living love
For one to whom I made it o'er his grave   35
Sacred, accept this old imperfect tale,
New-old, and shadowing Sense at war with Soul
Rather than that gray king, whose name, a ghost,
Streams like a cloud, man-shaped, from mountain peak,
And cleaves to cairn and cromlech still; or him   40
Of Geoffrey's book, or him of Malleor's, one
Touch'd by the adulterous finger of a time
That hover'd between war and wantonness,
And crownings and dethronements: take withal
Thy poet's blessing, and his trust that Heaven   4 ?
Will blow the tempest in the distance back
From thine and ours: for some are scared, who mark,
Or wisely or unwisely, signs of storm,
Waverings of every vane with every wind,
And wordy trucklings to the transient hour,   50
And fierce or careless looseners of the faith,
And Softness breeding scorn of simple life,
Or Cowardice, the child of lust for gold,
Or Labor, with a groan and not a voice,
Or Art with poisonous honey stol'n from France,   55
And that which knows, but careful for itself,
And that which knows not, ruling that which knows
To its own harm: the goal of this great world
Lies beyond sight: yet — if our slowly-grown
And crown'd Republic's crowning common-sense,   60
That saved her many times, not fail — their fears
Are morning shadows huger than the shapes
That cast them, not those gloomier which forego
The darkness of that battle in the West,
Where all of high and holy dies away.   65

NOTES

In Twelve Books. Twelve books is the number in the two great epics best known to modern readers: Virgil's *Æneid* and Milton's *Paradise Lost*. Twelve was also the number of books planned by Spenser for his *Faerie Queene*, though he completed only six of them, and a little of the seventh.

Flos Regum Arthurus. Arthur, the flower of kings.

DEDICATION

LINE

1 **His Memory.** To the memory of Prince Albert, the husband of Queen Victoria. He died in December, 1861. The volume of the Idylls containing *The Coming of Arthur*, *The Holy Grail*, *Pelleas and Ettare*, and *The Passing of Arthur* was published in 1869.

12 **Imminent war.** An allusion, probably, to the danger of war, late in 1861, between England and the United States, caused by "the Trent affair." See any history of the United States; for example, Fiske's.

35 **The rich dawn of an ampler day.** In reference to the many new discoveries in science, and new ideas of the nineteenth century. Compare *Locksley Hall*.

36–7 **Summoner of War and Waste,** etc. Prince Albert had arranged the great International Exposition at London in 1851, and was at work on the second, that of 1862, at the time of his death.

47 **Has past.** The subject of this verb is "that star," in line 45.

THE COMING OF ARTHUR

1 **Cameliard,** an unidentified region, seemingly in southeast England.

5 **Petty king.** Britain was divided into many tribes or

clans, the " king " of each being no more than a sort of chief.

8 **Heathen host.** The Angles and the Saxons, who made invasions and settlements in Britain in the fifth and sixth centuries.

13 **Aurelius,** " a descendant of the last Roman general who claimed the purple as an emperor of Britain." — Green, *The Making of England.*

32 **Wolf-like men.** Stories of children nourished by wolves, and growing up into " wolf-like men " were common and widespread. Compare the story of Romulus and Remus. See an unabridged dictionary for the term *were-wolves.*

34 **Roman legions.** The part of Britain that is now England had been invaded and conquered by Cæsar in the first century, B.C. The Romans maintained their power there, and exacted tribute of the Britons for four or five centuries.

36 **Urien,** according to Malory, was a king of North Wales " who made great war upon Leodogrance, king of Cameliard."

43 **Uther's son.** According to Malory, Uther Pendragon, a king in southern Britain, fell in love with Igraine, or Ygerne, wife of Gorlois, Duke of Tintagil in Cornwall; made war upon Gorlois, slew him, and married Igraine in the castle of Tintagil, where she had taken refuge. Of this union Arthur was born. In accordance with the old Celtic custom of fosterage, and to save the child's life, he was given over to Merlin immediately after his birth, and given by Merlin to the wife of Sir Ector to be reared. See Tennyson's version of the story in lines 184–236.

50 **Kinglihood,** kingship.

73 **Anton,** in one of the old stories (not Malory's) is the knight in whose family Arthur is brought up.

LINE

96 **Pavilions.** Tents. To " pitch " a tent is to set it up.

102 **Shrilling unto blood.** Stirring the blood.

103 **The long-lanced battle, . . . run.** That is, the lines of battle rode against each other.

105 **The King.** King Arthur.

106 **The Powers.** The supernatural powers.

111–5 This list of kings is borrowed from Malory, I, 10.

116–8 **One who sees,** etc. That is, one who has his sin discovered and proclaimed.

119 **To stay the brands,** etc. To stop fighting.

124–5 **Warrior whom he loved and honored most.** Sir Launcelot. See lines 446–7.

127 **Liege** is an old word, common in poetry, meaning one to whom are due service and allegiance, or faithful loyalty.

132 **Man's word is God in man.** That is, man's word, or promise, is a sacred thing.

134 **Foughten.** This old form of the participle still survives in the word *boughten*, especially in New England.

141 **Holp,** an old form of the verb, like *tell, told; sell, sold.*

150 **Merlin,** the wise man, the magician, appears many times in the Idylls and in the various versions of the Arthurian legends. He had not only great knowledge, but the gifts of prophecy and magic.

160 **Holpen.** See notes on lines 134 and 141.

160–2 Note the king's way of telling the old man his knowledge is useless.

167 **And reason in the chase.** The cuckoo lays its eggs in the nests of other birds, to be hatched, after throwing out the eggs of the owners of the nest.

177 **Be.** This is an old use of the verb, still found in many parts of England and New England.

183 **So.** An old use of the word, equivalent to *if*.

187 Note the alliteration in this line.

191–2 The pronouns refer to Ygerne, not to Bellicent.

LINE

194 Bright dishonor. A distinction, yet dishonorable.

203–4 This is one of the many instances in which Tennyson assigns the taste and morals of his own century to the period of King Arthur. In Malory the knights and ladies are much less sensitive to such improprieties.

214–20 Tennyson here supplies a reason for the secret bringing up of Arthur. See note on line 43. See also the story of Arthur's birth in Tennyson's *Guinevere*, lines 282–93.

227 His hour. Whose hour? Merlin's, or Arthur's?

230–3 According to Malory, the true king was to be he who could draw a certain sword from a stone in which it was deeply thrust. All the kings and nobles tried, but only Arthur could withdraw it. The people clamored for him to be their king, and he was crowned by the Archbishop of Canterbury. Compare the story of Siegfreid and the sword.

252 Body enow. Weight enough, power enough.

256 Uther's peerage. The knights and kings under Uther.

257 Dais. A low platform on which the king's chair stood.

261 Strait. Narrow, strict.

262 Knighted from kneeling. In the old ceremony the candidate for knighthood knelt before the king, who struck him gently on the shoulder with the flat side of the sword and said, "Arise, Sir John," or whatever name the knight bore. This stroke of the sword admitting to knighthood, was called an *accolade*.

266 Table Round. The "round table," from which the order of King Arthur and his knights was named, was a custom of the early Britons or Celts. The place nearest the salt was the place of favor, or of honor. If the guests sat at equal distance from the salt, at the center, there could be no quarrels on this point.

271–4 "The cross," etc. . . . This passage seems to describe pictures and Christian symbols in stained glass. But stained glass was first made long after the date ascribed to King Arthur. Tennyson cares more for beauty of picture than for historical accuracy.

275 **Three fair queens.** Perhaps the same three queens who appear at Arthur's death, and bear him in the barge across the lake. See *The Passing of Arthur*, lines 361, and following. Do they symbolize anything? Perhaps the Christian virtues, Faith, Hope, and Charity. See Tennyson's own comment in the *Introduction*, page 12.

282 **The Lady of the Lake.** Commonly understood to symbolize the Church, as Tennyson uses her. In the original story (see Malory, I, xxii) she is a mystical lady who gives Arthur the magic sword, Excalibur.

288 **Minster.** A cathedral which had its origin in a monastery, of which word *minster* is a corruption.

293 **To walk the waters like our Lord.** So Malory describes her: "They saw a damsel going upon the lake." The comparison is to the miracle told in Matt. xiv, and Mark vi.

298 **Urim.** Flames or lights. (A Hebrew plural, indicated by the termination *im*. Compare the words *seraphim* and *cherubim*.) The *Urim* were worn in the breastplate of the high priest of the Jews. They are thought to have been small figures or jewels, of some mystic or sacred significance. But what they were is not certainly known. At any rate, they fit in well enough with the rest of the mystery of this poem. The word occurs in Ex. xxviii, Lev. viii, and Num. xxvii.

301 **The oldest tongue of all this world.** What this is no one knows. But note the effect of mystery and wonder which the line suggests. Tennyson, of course, means that the words were in Hebrew.

310 **To sift his doubtings.** How would this be expressed in everyday English?

318 To pass. To withdraw.

322 Modred's stealthy and treacherous nature appears elsewhere in the *Idylls: Guinevere,* 10–110; *The Passing of Arthur,* 10–50, 150–70.

332 The dawning of my life. My infancy.

342 Heath. The heath or heather is a small, shrubby plant growing in great abundance on the moors and other waste land of Great Britain. It has a small bell-shaped flower, commonly purple, but sometimes pink or white.

362 Shrunk like a fairy changeling. There was an old belief that fairies sometimes carried off infants and left little elves in their stead. These were called *changelings* and were sometimes known by their old and shriveled appearance.

371 What kind of night does this mean?

372–93 This story of the coming of the babe Arthur is an excellent example of the wild yet childlike imagination of the people of the Middle Ages.

380 Full of voices. There is a likeness between the sound of waves and the murmur of many voices.

402–10 What is the general meaning of Merlin's "riddling triplets"?

407 Truth or clothed or naked. Truth told in parables or by symbols or embellished; — truth told barely or simply.

410 From the great deep to the great deep. From the unknown past into eternity.

421 Again to come. In Malory, XXI, 7, it is said that many thought that Arthur was not dead, and that he would come again.

426–43 Read the king's dream carefully. What does it mean? What other significant dreams have you read in old stories?

431 The hind fell, the herd was driven: The peasants were killed, and their cattle driven away as plunder.

LINE

450 This, the first of the *Idylls*, and *Gareth and Lynette*, the second in the series, are laid in the spring of the year. The last two, *Guinevere* and *The Passing of Arthur* are in the winter, the end of the year. See *Introduction*, p. 15.

452 **To whom arrived.** To whom, when she arrived, the king was married by Dubric, etc.

460 **White with May.** A kind of hawthorn, with a profuse white bloom, called the may.

476 **Great lords from Rome,** come to demand their annual tribute of the Britons. See the answer that they get from Arthur, lines 506–13.

481–501 In this lyric notice how often Tennyson has used repetition with slight variations. Note also the martial clang and ring that the song has; the harsh and rugged music of it.

504 **Rome, the slow-fading mistress of the world.** By the sixth or seventh century Rome, weakened by the invasions of the barbarians from the North, was rapidly losing her great power.

508 **The old order changeth,** etc. This line occurs again near the end of *The Passing of Arthur*, line 408. It is an idea that Tennyson has expressed in many places.

513 **Strove with Rome.** Was at enmity, but not at war, with Rome.

514–5 **For a space,** etc. This is a forecast of the trouble and disunion that later interfere with Arthur's work, and finally destroy both Round Table and kingdom.

516–8 Arthur's achievement was to unify the land into one kingdom by making the petty kings his vassals; to drive back the heathen (the Teutonic invaders); to purge the land of robbers and wild beasts; and to uphold order, law, and religion.

GARETH AND LYNETTE

Gareth and Lynette, though it follows *The Coming of Arthur* in the series of the Idylls, was not written until the end, in 1872.

LINE

18 **Heaven yield her.** Heaven reward her.

46 **Book of Hours.** A book of devotions, with prayers for the hours of the day.

66 **Excalibur.** Arthur's sword. The swords of heroes were often given individual names.

89 **Frights.** Explain the construction here.

94 **Prone year.** Declining life.

105 **Good lack.** Alas.

115–118 Commit to memory these well-known lines.

128 Recall the doubts concerning Arthur's birth as told in *The Coming of Arthur.*

133–4 Where is this described?

147 Point out the play on words here.

174 Note the imaginative quality in this line.

184–93 The city is made to seem mysterious here and later.

202 **Glamour.** Enchantment. Look up the origin of this word in the dictionary.

212 **The Lady of the Lake.** A mythical personage, a guardian to Arthur.

219 **The sacred fish.** An emblem of the Church, said to be derived from the accidental fact that the initials of the Greek words for Jesus Christ, Son of God, Savior, happened to form the Greek word meaning fish. Ask your teacher to write out the Greek for you.

229 **Dragon-boughts.** A bought is a loop or curve.

254–74 Study this passage carefully. The city "built to music" is an old Greek idea. Troy was fabled to have taken form under Apollo's music, and the wall around Thebes rose to Amphion's lyre.

For the idea in the last lines, remember that Camelot was a city of ideals, that ideals are never perfectly realized, that they are ever growing, and that they endure forever.

298 Did their days in stone. Had the record of their deeds carved in stone.

355 Wreak. Avenge.

366 Had doom'd. Subjunctive form; compare the verb in the next line.

380 Charlock. Wild mustard. What color is it?

405 Blazon'd. Drawn in colors.

422 In cloth of lead. Lead was used for coffins.

465 Sir Fair-hands. In Malory, Kay gives Gareth the nickname of Beau-Mains.

476 Broach. A spit, a sharp iron rod on which the meat was held while roasting.

529 News. Note the old plural form. Compare the French word for news, *nouvelles*.

607 A holy life. The life of a nun or monk.

657 Counter to. Opposite.

665 A maiden shield. A shield undecorated with exploits.

693 Hath past his time. Is falling into dotage.

729 Agaric. Mushroom. **Holt.** Grove or orchard.

784-5 Note the antithetic use of words here and in 787-8.

873 Ruth. Pity. From what verb is the noun derived?

881-2 To what is the allusion?

972 Unhappiness. Mishap, accident.

1002-3 What flower is meant?

1012 Vizoring up. Putting up the vizor of his helmet.

1023-5 Note the peculiar involved construction here, equivalent to, He fought no more and yielded.

1101-4 Here we have a hint of the allegory further described in lines 1167-79.

1130 Look back over the lyrics that Lynette has sung, and see how they indicate her change of view toward Gareth.

LINE

1281 **Arthur's Harp.** In *The Last Tournament* there is a passage, "the star we call the harp of Arthur up in Heaven."

1318 **Instant.** Urgent, impressive.

1373 Going back to the allegory in 1167–79, what do you make of Tennyson's meaning here? If a man has won the battles for good in the morning, the noon, and the evening of his life, what will death be to him? A thing to be feared, or the entrance to a new and beautiful life? Compare lines 1388–90.

1392–4 Which ending would have pleased you best?

As for the place of this Idyll in the series, note the conflict between the better and the worse ideals, first between Gareth and his mother, then between Gareth and Lynette. Which prevails? What evidences are there at the Court that the good influences are in control?

What passages of striking beauty can you find? Do you think of Lynette as a medieval or a modern girl? Does Gareth seem near or remote?

LANCELOT AND ELAINE

This Idyll shows openly the growing evil in the Court of Arthur. The indirect cause of Elaine's death is Lancelot's guilty love of Guinevere. It is not allegorical, like *Gareth and Lynette;* but a romantic story of a passion which, though pure and innocent, transcends ordinary bounds. It is therefore not to be read for an ethical lesson, but for its beauty and its pathos.

Read first *The Lady of Shalott,* Tennyson's early version of the story, wherein he pictures the heroine as a type of the artistic imagination weaving into the web the figures of the world as she sees them in the mirror (her imagination).

LINE

2 **Astolat.** Used in Malory. Compare Shalott.

44 **Lichen'd.** Covered with dry moss.

53 **Shingly scaur.** Rock covered with gravel (or shingle).

59 **Divinely.** By divine direction. Providentially.

76 **This world's hugest.** London.

91 **The tale.** The number.

94 **Lets.** Hinders, keeps.

118 **Devoir.** Duty; a French word.

162 **Downs.** Rolling hills of thin soil and sparse vegetation.

218 **An if.** *An* alone is also used for *if*.

272 **Reft.** Deprived.

293 **Our Lady's Head.** An image of the Virgin Mary.

297 **The White Horse** was a symbol of the Saxons. On a hillside in Berkshire there may still be seen the image of a huge white horse made by uncovering the chalky rock of the hill. It is said to have been made by King Alfred in memory of a victory over the Danes.

301 **Heathen.** The Saxons and Danes became Christians later than the British.

325 **To make him cheer.** To show him kindness.

331–4 Explain these lines.

338 **Rathe.** Early. *Rather* is the comparative degree.

431 **Samite.** A kind of heavy silk.

446 **Crescent.** Growing, increasing in power.

453 **Held the lists.** Awaited the attack. The *lists* was the enclosure within which the combat was fought.

502 **Diamond me,** etc. Note here and in line 505 the noun as verb. What do these lines mean?

545 **Bring us,** etc. Bring us news of where he is.

652–3 To "slip" the falcon was to release it from the holding-strings, that it might bring down the game in its flight.

713 A famous line, often quoted.

728 **Marr'd her friend's aim,** etc. Did not betray her emotion, as her friend had expected.

766 Wit ye well. Know you well.

870–2 Another well-known passage. Explain it.

905 The victim's flowers. An animal sacrificed at the altar was thus bedecked.

923 Is yours. Is your doing, is due to your kindness.

939 Quit. Requite, repay.

999 Make. Compose poetry. Our word *poet* is from a Greek word meaning *maker*.

1000–11 Note the rhyme arrangement.

1015–6. A common belief. In Ireland such a spirit is called a Banshee.

1092 The ghostly man. The priest.

1233–1410 Compare with this account the brief and simple ending of *The Lady of Shalott*.

1418 Die a holy man. The end of Lancelot's life was spent in prayer and penance in a monastery.

THE HOLY GRAIL

The Holy Grail was first printed, with *The Coming of Arthur*, in 1869.

5 **The cowl** was the hood attached to the gown worn by the monks.

7 **Camelot.** The city where lived King Arthur and his knights.

10 **Wrought into his heart,** etc. Won the love of Percivale by showing his own love for him.

14 **The cloisters.** The arched and covered way running around the walls of a monastery, or convent, usually on the inner court.

15 **That puff'd the swaying branches into smoke.** The pollen of the yew-tree, when scattered by the wind, resembles smoke.

21 **Beyond the pale.** Beyond the limits of the monastery.

LINE

33 **Earthly heats.** Earthly passions.

38 **Green in Heaven's eyes,** etc. That is, alive to things spiritual or religious, though too much dead to the world beyond our walls.

41 **Refectory.** The common name for the dining-hall in convents, monasteries, and Catholic schools.

47 **His own.** His disciples.

48 **Aromat,** a poetic form, for Arimathea, the home of that Joseph who placed Jesus in his own sepulcher. According to the mediæval legend Joseph had received in the cup (the Grail) the blood that flowed from the side of Jesus when pierced by the spear.

49 **The day of darkness,** etc. The day was darkened, an earthquake came, and the graves gave up their dead at the death of Jesus. Moriah was the name of the hill on which the temple of Jerusalem was built. See Matt. XXVII, 50 *ff.*

52 **Glastonbury.** The first church and first monastery were said to have been built here. Here King Arthur was said to be buried. The abbey was several times destroyed and rebuilt, the last time under Henry II, in the twelfth century.

54 **It bode.** This refers, of course, to the Grail.

61 **Arviragus,** according to the legends, was a king of Britain in the first century A.D. He is mentioned in Shakespeare's *Cymbeline.*

63 **Wattles.** Framework made of rods or twigs interwoven.

67 **To-day.** Used here in the sense of *in our day.*

73 This line is parenthetical, and might have been set off by dashes or marks of parentheses.

75 **Rudely blunted,** etc. Disappointed in love, she turned to the religious life.

78 **The scandal of the court.** The rumor of the guilty love of Lancelot and Queen Guinevere.

LINE

81 Across ... beat. Reached even to the solitude of her convent.

83 He to whom, etc. Her father confessor.

91 He. The priest referred to in line 83.

93 That it would come. Note this manner of expressing an earnest wish.

110 Use. Custom, habit.

114 Nor aught ... hand. No sort of musical instrument.

118 Beatings. A throbbing or quivering effect, so that the colors on the wall seemed to leap (line 120).

122 Decay'd. Faded.

124 So now (that) **the Holy Thing,** etc.

135 White armor. A symbol of his perfect purity.

151 Made a silken matwork for her feet. Reached below her feet.

155 A silver beam. A band of silver.

169–70 In and out (among) **the figures,** etc.

172 Siege. An old word for *seat.*

181 Would. Here used to express determination.

183 Riving. Splitting, tearing, rending.

188 Stole. Moved gently.

190 Past. Disappeared.

209 Crying on help. Crying for help.

211 Red-rent. Explain this expression.

214–5 Explain the meaning of this figure of speech. See lines 264–6.

221 Smitten by the bolt. It was an old belief, still sometimes held, that an actual bolt or missile of some sort comes with the lightning flash. In classic myth, it was Zeus or Jupiter hurling his "thunderbolt"; in Norse myth, it was Thor striking with his mighty hammer.

232 Zones. Rows, belts.

234–7 Note that these sculptured devices indicate the rise of men from barbarism to civilization. Lines 227–45, you

LINE

will observe, describe the city and the outside of the
hall. The passage that follows describes the inside of the
hall.

248 **Blazon.** Celebrate, commemorate.

252–3 Describing the scene told in *The Coming of Arthur*,
lines 282–308.

254–7 The scene that is to be enacted later. See *The Passing
of Arthur*, lines 361–440.

260 **Dreamlike.** Fanciful and beautiful, like a dream.

263 **The golden dragon** on the crest of the king's helmet.

264 **Burnt the hold.** Burnt the place where the robbers
were; line 214.

267 **Prest.** The subject of this verb is *many*, line 264.

275 **Darken.** The sentence is made clear by reading this
verb as after *seen it* in line 273.

287 This line is adapted from Matt. xi, 7.

298 The king's speech breaks off here with an unfinished
sentence. Then he begins in line 300 with an illustration of his meaning.

300 **Taliessin.** A Welsh bard, supposed to be of the
sixth century, and attached to the court of the son
of King Urien. Some of his poems are still in exist-
ence.

301 **The dumb will sing.** That is, will try to sing, or wish to
sing.

312 **The White Horse** was the emblem of the Saxons, "the
heathen horde."

314 The sacredness of a vow is a common thing in the earlier
literatures. Recall Arthur's saying, " Man's word is
God in man," *The Coming of Arthur*, line 132.

319–20 **Wandering fires . . . quagmire.** The will-o'-the-
wisp, which hovers over marshy places, was fabled to
entice people to their death.

340–50 Note the highly *mediæval* quality given to the archi-
tecture of Camelot; the crowded roofs, the galleries or

LINE

    balconies resting on images of dragons, and the carv-
ings of dragons, lions, etc., with which the houses
were ornamented.

350 **Wyvern, griffin.** See a dictionary for these heraldic
devices.

375–540 This passage, a succession of visions, gives the very
quality of the search for the Grail, itself a vision. Indeed, this entire Idyll creates the impression of moving in dreamland, the reveries and memories of the
mystery-loving Sir Percivale. Note how the kindly,
simple, everyday life of the good monk Ambrosius
serves as contrast and background for the dreams of
Percivale.

447–8 In reference to the incarnation of the Lord.

449 **She.** The pronoun refers to humility, line 445.

452–3 See in Matt. II, the story of the coming of the wise
men of the East to see the infant Christ.

462–3 **The sacring of the mass.** The consecration of the
bread and wine used in the celebration of the mass. The
holy elements are the bread and wine, believed to symbolize the flesh and blood of Christ.

466–7 After the belief that Christ, or the spirit of Christ,
actually entered the bread and wine.

470–84 Compare this passage with Tennyson's short poem,
Galahad, written many years earlier.

512–3 **The Holy Vessel,** etc. The Grail.

525 **The waste.** The swamp; see line 499.

526 **The spiritual city.** A symbol, at least, of Paradise.

542 and 545 Each of these lines is parenthetic.

547 **Thorpe.** Village.

550–60 Note how these lines express the simple, kindly
nature of the old monk. He is introduced as a contrast
to the knights, who pursued the vision of the Grail.
Note his significant question in lines 561–2. The "market-cross," line 558, means a cross set up in the central

square, or market-place of a town; they still exist in many English towns.

574–5 Disarmed by maidens, etc. This hospitable custom is often mentioned in the stories of chivalry.

580 A slender page. As a training for the duties and graces of knighthood, the young sons of nobles often served as pages in the house of some knight or prince.

612 When yule is cold. When the yule log, the center of the Christmas festivities, is burnt out.

614 So that. If.

628 Earth. The hole in the earth, the lair, of badger or of fox.

633 The pelican on the casque. The image of some animal or bird worn on the helmet was a common badge or emblem.

639 Maddening what he rode. Urging his horse to the point of madness.

657 With small adventure met. Having met with few adventures.

659–64 In reference to the Druids, remnants of the ancient Celtic people. Ruins of their old places of worship may still be seen in England, notably at Stonehenge, near Salisbury. These temples were several circles of huge upright stones, open to the sky, with a central stone or altar, the whole so arranged as to indicate a knowledge of the recurrent positions of the sun.

667–9 The Druids were supposed to be worshipers of the sun, as these lines indicate.

679 The streaming scud. Light clouds and rain.

681 The seven clear stars. The constellation of the Great Bear, near the North Star; often called in this country "the dipper," because of the shape of the group.

706 Sooth. Truth.

710–12 Such words as those of Lancelot and the king are not lightly forgotten.

LINE

714–6 Unicorns . . . talbots. Heraldic emblems, of stone, set in houses; but here fallen in the street, and indicating the neglect and approaching ruin of Camelot.

725 Flooding ford. A ford is a shallow place in a river, used for crossing, when there is no bridge. In times of high water, or "in flood," such fords may be dangerous.

759–60 Of Cana in Holy Writ. In allusion to the miracle of the turning of the water into wine. See John II.

777 They. The good and the evil.

790 Folly. Madness. See lines 666–7.

808 Shingle. The gravel on the beach.

810 Carbonek. The name is from Malory.

821–2 Compare the use of the lions in the path in Bunyan's *Pilgrim's Progress*.

828 Oriel. A small room or portico projecting from a building.

848–9 Why did Lancelot only see the Grail veiled?

862 Deafer than the blue-eyed cat. A superstition that still exists.

865 *ff.* Note that Arthur, though he has not approved of the quest of the Grail (see lines 293 *ff.*), rebukes Gawain for his levity, and commends the other knights for their serious attitude towards sacred things.

872–5 Every prophet and every poet, though conveying God's message, could prophesy or sing it only in the measure of their ability.

877–83 Arthur means that if a man did wrong, and yet kept alive some fine feelings and some ideals, even about his sin, he could not become wholly base.

884–915 In this passage Tennyson puts into the mouth of Arthur his own code of morality. For most of us, as for most of the knights of the Round Table, it is not best to follow vague ideals, "wandering fires," no matter by what noble ideals we may be inspired. Our duty is here and now, in the work and human needs that are near at hand.

908–10 Remember that in Percivale's quest, almost all that he saw were mere phantoms, delusions. Even Lancelot drove on in madness. Yet to Bors, the sane and sturdy and faithful, the Grail came also. And what seems a vision may be real, when one

> knows himself no vision to himself,
> Nor the high God a vision, nor that One
> Who rose again: ye have seen what ye have seen.

916 Percivale's closing words, "I knew not all he meant," seem to give us the right to feel that some of the king's high and oracular utterances may be understood dimly or in various ways.

THE PASSING OF ARTHUR

The Passing of Arthur was first published, in its present form, in the volume with *The Coming of Arthur*, in 1869. It is an enlargement, with some changes, of the *Morte d'Arthur*, published in 1842 in the volume *English Idylls*. The main part of the story of this Idyll is taken from Malory, xxi, v. This last division of Malory's account is called *La Morte d'Arthur* or *The Death of Arthur*.

1–5 **That story:** meaning, This is that story, etc.

3 **The man was no more than a voice.** Meaning?

6 **On their march,** etc. This Idyll opens at a time when the Round Table is dissolved, and war has broken out. A part of the knights are still faithful to the king, and the rest, led by Modred and Lancelot, are at war with King Arthur.

22 **Simple.** Trustful, believing.

LINE

26 **Reels back into the beast.** Becomes fierce and degraded again. Why *reels?*

33 **Shrilling.** Tennyson seems to like the weird effect of this word. See how many times you find it, either as verb or adjective, in this poem. **Hollow all delight!** All joy is empty and fleeting.

38–40 **Wild birds that change their season,** etc. Some of the migratory birds that go north in spring and south in autumn fly high, and travel day and night. Read Bryant's poem, *To a Waterfowl.*

42 **Moonlit haze among the hills.** Do you get the picture?

44–5 **Wife and Child,** etc. In olden times the women and children of the conquered were often carried off into slavery by the victors.

52 **Harmless glamour of the field.** The imaginary beings in nature.

68–70 These are the events told of in *The Coming of Arthur.*

77 In reference to Queen Guinevere, who had taken refuge in the convent at Almesbury, and to whom Arthur had there said good-bye. See the Idyll, *Guinevere,* lines 410 *ff.*

78 **Folded in the passes of the world.** Closed the way as by a mist or darkness.

81 **Lyonnesse.** A district supposed to lie between Cornwall and the Scilly Islands, and now submerged.

82–7 A land made by volcanic action. Note the boldness of imagination in this picture.

87 **The phantom circle.** The dim line of the horizon, between sea and sky.

90–1 **The shortest day of the year.** As the events of the early days of Arthur's reign have spring as their setting, so his death has the end of the year and a winter landscape for its appropriate background.

LINE

94 **Dim, weird battle.** What things in this whole paragraph, lines 79–118, make the scene *dim* and *weird?*

108-10 Read these lines aloud, and note how they suggest the shock and crash of fighting.

113-7 Does Tennyson here make war seem glorious? Or is it made to seem bestial?

119 **Or thro' death, or,** etc. Either through death or, etc.

121 **Seething.** Surging and chafing, as if boiling.

127 **No man was moving there.** Is this forceful? Why?

129 *ff.* Remember that Arthur's army had overtaken the enemy on the coast, and fought them there; and then "with the wind the tide rose," and so flowed in among the dead.

133 **Once had fought with Rome.** A reminder of the days in which they fought together against a foreign enemy.

134-5 What do these lines suggest? The ceaseless movement and roar of the sea?

139 **This great voice,** etc. The roaring waves that beat upon the land and wear it down.

151-2 **But (he) who hates thee, and who
Brought the heathen back among us.**
Made allies of the heathen (the Saxons) in his war against Arthur.

154 **My house hath been my doom.** Modred was Arthur's half-brother. He and Queen Guinevere were the two that had most injured the king.

169 These first lines, (1–169), were added in 1869 to the first version of the Idyll, the *Morte d'Arthur* of 1842. It is not quite clear how the single combat, just told of, comes in. Is it in a pause in the battle? But all was quiet; see lines 127-31.

170 In the *Introduction* to this poem, in the 1842 version, the poem is supposed to be read aloud by the poet to a group of friends. Notice how often, as in 171-2, the lines have a deep, sonorous quality.

LINE

172 The name "*King Arthur's Table*," or "seat," has been applied to a hill near Tintagil, in Cornwall.

177 **Chancel.** The inclosed part of the church in which the altar stands. Notice the beautiful and romantic scene in lines 177-80.

198-9 Where have you read these lines before?

205 **The middle mere.** The middle of the lake.

206 **Lightly.** Quickly.

211 **Hest.** Behest, command.

213-9 Note the weird beauty of this picture, and how, in the last two lines, we get a feeling of the change in both sound and scene.

220-30. Note the richness and beauty of these lines.

228 **This way and that dividing the swift mind.** Students who know Latin may find that this line is a translation of *Æneid*, IV, 285, which Virgil had borrowed from Homer's *Iliad*, I, 188-9. Tennyson greatly admired Virgil, and wrote a beautiful poem *To Virgil* in praise of him.

238-9. Test the sound of these lines. Does it suggest the things described?

252 **The dewy pebbles.** The gems in the hilt.

254 **Chased.** Wrought, ornamented.

256 *ff.* Why does Sir Bedivere argue these points with himself?

276 **Winning reverence** by the wonder and interest of the tale he told.

278 **Clouded with his own conceit.** Blinded by the idea that had come to him.

289 **Authority forgets a dying king.** What does this fine line mean? Explain the rest of the sentence.

293 **Offices.** Services, duties.

304-15 Another of those rich and brilliant passages. **The northern moon.** *Aurora borealis* or "northern lights."

350-1 Get the picture in these lines clearly.

354-60 Read these lines aloud, clearly and vigorously.

LINE

Note again the rugged harshness and energy of the passage sliding off, at the end, into the smoother beauty of the last two lines.

367 **The tingling stars.** Twinkling, trembling as though affected by the agony of the cry. The same idea is suggested in *shivered*.

369-71 What is the feeling inspired by these lines?

381 Why *withered* moon?

382 **The springing east.** The early dawn.

383 **Greaves and cuisses.** Armor for the legs: greaves below the knee, cuisses above.

384 **Onset.** Conflict.

398 **Chance.** Happening.

400-1 The Star of Bethlehem that guided the Wise Men of the East to where the infant Jesus lay. See Matt. II.

408-10 New customs, new standards and ideals, come to take the place of the old; and God works out his purposes in many ways. Even a good plan may come to be misused, and a good institution grow corrupt.

422-3 Explain these lines.

427 **Avilion** (or Avalon) is, in Celtic legend, and as used by Tennyson, The Land of the Blest, a sort of earthly paradise in the western sea, like the Greek Hesperides. Not only Arthur but other heroes, like Ogier the Dane, were said to have been carried there after death. It is often called The Vale of Avalon.

435 The belief that the swan sings a beautiful song just before death was old and widespread. Hence the phrase, "swan song," for last effort.

442 **The dead world's winter dawn.** Note how this scene fits the ending of the story of Arthur.

457-61 What is hinted in this passage?

469 Does this line give a note of hope? Compare 408-10.

DEDICATION TO THE QUEEN

This dedication to the Queen was first added in the general edition of the Poems in 1872–73.

3 **That rememberable day.** The day of public thanksgiving, in February, 1872, for the recovery of the Prince of Wales (later King Edward VII) from a severe illness.

12 **Thunderless lightnings,** etc. Messages by cable.

14 **That true North,** etc. In reference to Canada, and a sentiment that was heard for a time in England that Canada should be separated from England.

20 **The roar of Hougoumont.** The battle of Waterloo. The château of that name was on the battlefield.

21 **Left mightiest,** etc. After the victory at Waterloo England was unquestionably the greatest power in the world.

35 **For one to whom I made it.** See the *Dedication* at the beginning of the *Idylls* in this volume.

37 **Shadowing Sense at war with Soul.** Picturing or reflecting the conflict between evil and good, between the lower and the higher ideals. This line is the keynote to the meaning of the *Idylls* as a whole. See *Introduction*, page 13.

41–2 In reference to the different qualities given to the stories in the different versions. See *Introduction*, pages 7–9.

55 **Poisonous honey stol'n from France.** Art and literature from France, which seemed to the poet to be unwholesome or immoral. Tennyson has more than once showed his lack of belief in things French or sympathy with them.

QUESTIONS AND TOPICS FOR STUDY

DEDICATION TO THE IDYLLS

1. To whom is this dedication addressed? What is a dedication of a book for? Have you ever seen one before? Sometimes a very brief dedication is printed on one of the pages of a book, between the title-page and the first page of the preface.

2. Explain the meaning of lines 2 and 3.

3. Look up the rest of the quotation begun in line 7. You will find it in *Guinevere*, lines 464–480. It is a famous expression of the finest ideals of chivalry.

4. What high qualities does Tennyson ascribe to Prince Albert? Commit to memory lines 24–27. Explain the meaning of lines 27–29; of lines 30–33. See in the Notes the explanation of line 35.

5. Does this *Dedication* seem extravagant in its adulation of royalty?

THE COMING OF ARTHUR

1. Note how the story is begun. The first paragraph tells who Guinevere was. The second paragraph begins the account of the state of the country before Arthur came, and the fourth tells how Leodogran summoned Arthur to help him. The fifth paragraph tells of Arthur's love for Guinevere; the fourth and sixth tell of the doubts about Arthur's right to be king. These two themes, introduced side by side, are the main themes of this Idyll.

2. What was the state of the country before Arthur triumphed? What troubles and what enemies were there? Why were the Roman legions " groaned for "?

3. Who was King Uther, and why did it matter whether Arthur was or was not his son?

4. What is the " golden symbol " referred to in line 50 ?

5. Read aloud lines 94–123, to feel the vigor and spirit in this account of the battle.

6. Lines 124–133 give the vows of friendship between Arthur and Lancelot. Do you know how this friendship came later to be broken? If so, do you see the significance of introducing it here?

7. Why does Leodogran hesitate about giving his daughter to King Arthur? How does he seek to resolve his doubts? Explain lines 160–162.

8. Why the different opinions of Arthur's worth, in lines 178–182?

9. Sir Bedivere, commonly called " the bold Sir Bedivere," gives the true account of Arthur's birth. It is he who is with Arthur at his death: see *The Passing of Arthur*. See in the Notes the explanations of various things in Bedivere's story, lines 177–236.

10. Explain lines 245–6; line 247; line 252.

11. What is meant by "the savage yells of Uther's peerage," lines 255–6?

12. What evidence does Bellicent give of Arthur's moral force? See lines 259–278. Why did the knights have "a momentary likeness of the King "? What visions appeared? Read lines 279–293 aloud, the better to appreciate the rhythm of the verse.

13. What doubt still remains in Leodogran's mind? Does his doubt seem reasonable, or does Tennyson merely make him doubt further for the sake of bringing out the story of Arthur?

14. Note the traits of Bellicent's two sons: how are they shown?

15. What memory is indicated in lines 331–335?

16. Read aloud, for the rhythm and the beauty of de-

scription, Bellicent's memories of her childhood with her brother, lines 338–357.

17. How does her account of the birth of Arthur, which she received from old Bleys, the magician, differ from Bedivere's account? Which account seems the more credible? Would Leodogran have doubted a story merely because it was marvelous? Would you?

18. How had Merlin answered her questions? What do his " riddling triplets " mean?

19. Read aloud lines 411–423. Note how the verse rises in dignity as the Queen rises into prophecy of the coming fame of Arthur.

20. What finally banishes Leodogran's doubts? Is it in keeping with the time that he should think his dream significant and trustworthy? What other instances of belief in dreams can you recall? Select some of the finest lines in this dream.

21. Select the most beautiful lines in this picture of Arthur's marriage, lines 449–474. Compare with this passage Tennyson's early short poem, *Sir Lancelot and Queen Guinevere.*

22. What former passage in this Idyll do lines 463–4 recall to you?

23. Read aloud the triumphant battle-song of the knights, lines 481–501. Note the use of repetition; of harsh battle-like sounds; and the rough, staccato effects of the rhythm.

24. What is the meaning of the appearance here of the messengers from Rome and the way they are received?

25. How does the last scene in this Idyll bring our minds round to the beginning?

GARETH AND LYNETTE

1. Who was Gareth? Why did he remain at home?

2. What did he want to do? What kind of life did he wish to lead? Find passages that justify your answer.

3. Explain the parable in lines 98–114.

4. Quote lines 115–8, beginning "Man am I grown."

5. By what arguments does Gareth's mother try to dissuade him?

6. How did he win his mother's consent? What condition did she impose? Why?

7. Describe his departure, and his arrival at Camelot.

8. What were his first impressions of the city? Describe his meeting with Merlin.

9. Explain lines 254–274. Give, if you can, some parallel or instance of this truth from modern life.

10. What functions of King Arthur's Court does Gareth first see? What impressions of the King do they give you?

11. How is Gareth received by the King? Does any one suspect his disguise?

12. How is he treated by his master, Sir Kay? How by Lancelot?

13. How did he spend his time? How did he differ from his fellows?

14. What is his first quest?

15. What sort of girl does Lynette seem to be? How does she treat Gareth? Commit to memory lines 574–7.

16. What adventures does Gareth meet on the way? How does he acquit himself?

17. What allegory had been assumed in the armor of the men whom Gareth was to fight? See lines 1166 *ff*.

18. What is implied in the fact that the second combat is harder than the first, and the third fiercer still? See lines 1100–4.

19. What do the lyrics that Lynette sings mean? Show how they form a real part of the story.

20. What does the death's-head knight prove to be? What does this mean?

21. Where else have you read a description like that of the tournament in lines 1323–1345?

22. What does "fleshless laughter" (line 1348) mean?

23. How do you like the ending of the story?

24. What does the poem as a whole mean to you?

LANCELOT AND ELAINE

1. Note how the story opens in the middle, — *in medias res*, as it is called. Where does the author go back to the beginning?

2. What things are told about Elaine in the first paragraph?

3. Give an account of the origin of the "diamond jousts."

4. What was Lancelot's purpose in these tourneys? How did he happen to go unknown to this last one?

5. What does Guinevere say of Arthur? What impression has he made on you?

6. Who were in the household of Astolat? How do they receive Lancelot? Do they know who he is? What sort of face and manner had he?

7. Why does Lancelot wear Elaine's favor? Does any vestige of this old custom of chivalry still survive?

8. Compare the tournament here (lines 426–522) with that in *Ivanhoe*.

9. Whom does Arthur send in search of Lancelot? How does he perform his mission? How does Arthur rebuke him?

10. What indications of Guinevere's jealousy do you find?

11. What things in Elaine's life, her circumstances, and her character, seem to make her declaration of love less bold and unmaidenly than it might be in another?

12. Comment upon Lancelot's attitude towards her?

13. Why does she wish to be carried to Camelot after her death?

14. What do the people there think and say of her?

15. What things in the story put it in the land of pure romance?

16. How does this Idyll show the growing force of evil at the Court?

THE HOLY GRAIL

1. What was the Holy Grail? By what other name is it often known? To what kind of person only did it appear? What other literature do you know in which the Grail figures?

2. Sir Percivale had left the world and gone to be a monk in a monastery. How does Tennyson tell us this?

3. What picture is given in the second paragraph? Where are the two men? What are cloisters? What is the "smoke" of the yew-tree?

4. How had Ambrosius known whence Sir Percivale came? What does he know of the knights? How does he know of them?

5. What had brought Percivale to the monastery?

6. The old monk is curious about the story of the Grail; but to him it is only "the phantom of a cup that comes and goes." What is it to Percivale? What account of it does he give? What part of the story has Ambrosius already heard?

7. Who had first seen the vision of the Grail? What sort of person was she? What was "the scandal of the Court," line 78?

8. Read carefully the vision of the Grail as it appeared to Percivale's sister, lines 106–128. What use of color and sound does the poet make in this picture?

9. What is meant by "fasting"? What was the motive for it? Does the custom still exist?

10. Who had been most moved by the men's account of her vision? What sort of man was he? Read Tennyson's short poem, *Sir Galahad*. Explain lines 162–165.

11. What was "the Siege Perilous"? What was the legend about it?

12. What miraculous appearance set the knights upon the quest of the Grail? How did they regard a vow? Gawain made the vow, "and louder than the rest": what does Tennyson mean by this?

13. Why had not Arthur taken the vow? Would he have done so, if he had seen the vision of the Grail? What did he say when he found that so many of his knights had taken the vow? Why did he disapprove? Line 319 gives his phrase for the mistaken folly of the quest; remember it.

14. Study the descriptions of the hall and the city of Camelot. Pick out the beautiful and striking passages. Read aloud the following, for their beauty of picture and rhythm: lines 179–194; 205–224; 225–245; 258–270; 338–360.

15. In what spirit had Percivale begun the quest? See lines 361 ff. What doubts came later?

16. Beginning with line 379, Percivale recounts his experiences on his quest; which seem real and which seem like visions, mere phantoms of the mind? Did he ever see the Grail? See, especially, lines 489–539.

17. Read aloud the account of Galahad, 457–484.

18. What does Ambrosius think of all this realm of miracle and vision? What does he most like? Whom do you like best: Percivale, Galahad, or Ambrosius? Read aloud lines 540–563.

19. What episode of Percivale's earlier life was revived? How did he deal with it? What does Ambrosius think of his decision? What do you think of it? Read aloud 572–611; 612–631.

20. What happened to Sir Bors on the quest? What sort of man was Sir Bors?

21. Lancelot appears now and then in the poem: in what state of mind is he? Does he see the Grail?

22. Lines 708 to the end of the poem deal with the end of the quest. What changes are there in the city of Camelot? In the Round Table? What story has each knight to tell upon his return? How is the character of each shown by his experience?

23. Read aloud Lancelot's story, lines 763–849. What passages of beauty or strength do you find in it?

24. Why does Arthur rebuke Gawain? What is the meaning of his rebuke?

25. How again does Arthur show that the quest was a mistake? What do you think this Idyll, as a whole, means?

26. Tennyson's poem *The Palace of Art* will throw further light upon his meaning. Read it.

THE PASSING OF ARTHUR

1. The earlier form of this Idyll was published by Tennyson in 1842, under the title *Morte d'Arthur*. (See the Notes.) To this earlier version was prefixed the following Introduction:

THE EPIC

At Francis Allen's on the Christmas-eve, —
The game of forfeits done — the girls all kiss'd
Beneath the sacred bush and past away —
The parson Holmes, the poet Everard Hall,
The host, and I sat round the wassail-bowl,
Then half-way ebb'd: and there we held a talk,
How all the old honor had from Christmas gone,
Or gone, or dwindled down to some odd games
In some odd nooks like this; till I, tired out
With cutting eights that day upon the pond,
Where, three times slipping from the outer edge,
I bump'd the ice into three several stars,
Fell in a doze; and half awake I heard
The parson taking wide and wider sweeps,
Now harping on the church-commissioners,
Now hawking at Geology and schism;
Until I woke, and found him settled down
Upon the general decay of faith
Right thro' the world, "at home was little left,
And none abroad: there was no anchor, none,
To hold by." Francis, laughing, clapt his hand
On Everard's shoulder, with "I hold by him."
"And I," quoth Everard, "by the wassail-bowl."
"Why yes," I said, "we knew your gift that way
At college; but another which you had,
I mean of verse (for so we held it then),
What came of that?" "You know," said Frank, "he burnt
His epic, his King Arthur, some twelve books" —
And then to me demanding why? "Oh, sir,
He thought that nothing new was said, or else
Something so said 't was nothing — that a truth
Looks freshest in the fashion of the day:

God knows: he has a mint of reasons: ask.
It pleased *me* well enough." "Nay, nay," said Hall,
"Why take the style of those heroic times?
For nature brings not back the Mastodon,
Nor we those times; and why should any man
Remodel models? these twelve books of mine
Were faint Homeric echoes, nothing-worth,
Mere chaff and draff, much better burnt." "But I,"
Said Francis, "pick'd the eleventh from this hearth
And have it: keep a thing, its use will come.
I hoard it as a sugar-plum for Holmes."
He laugh'd, and I, tho' sleepy, like a horse
That hears the corn-bin open, prick'd my ears;
For I remember'd Everard's college fame
When we were Freshmen: then at my request
He brought it; and the poet little urged,
But with some prelude of disparagement,
Read, mouthing out his hollow oes and aes,
Deep-chested music, and to this result.

2. Sir Bedivere, " first made and latest left of all the knights," figures in *The Coming of Arthur*. Do you remember how?

3. Is the first paragraph (lines 1–5) a sentence? Or is it more like a title, or description, of what follows?

4. Is the use of *for*, line 6, like our use of it to-day? Could it be omitted here?

5. In lines 9–28, what is it that Arthur despairs of? What hopes had he entertained that have failed him? Explain lines 9–11.

6. Is there anything in the vision of Gawain's ghost that reminds you of Gawain living?

7. Explain the comparison in lines 38–40.

8. What lines in this paragraph (lines 29–49) give the sense of mystery or terror?

9. Why does the King feel such deep dejection?

10. Study the description beginning " the sunset bound of Lyonnesse." What was this country like?

11. What time of year is it? What is the season of the year at the end of *The Coming of Arthur?* What things in the scene and the season are in harmony with the King's dejection?

12. Read aloud lines 79–117. Select lines that are striking either for their rhythm or the picture they present.

Do such lines as 82, 85, 86, 92, 94, 95, move rapidly or slowly? What is the meaning of 82–3, 84, 87, 90–1? Note the striking effects in the description of the battle: the sense of confusion in the mist and darkness, the thoughts and memories that come to the fighters, the impression of crash and struggle and crude violence, the base passions and foul speech, the suffering and the grief. Taken as a whole, does this passage make war seem heroic or horrible? Read again lines 106 to 117, and notice the effect of the sound: how the passage gives the shock and crash of the fight, and the effect, at the end, of the cessation of sound and struggle.

13. In lines 120–1, note the effect of the *s* sounds: what are they intended to resemble?

14. What is the picture we get of the waves rising over the battlefield? See lines 127–135. Does this again make war seem heroic?

15. Read line 139. Note how slowly and laboringly it moves. What does this suggest to you? Compare the movement of it with that of line 141. What does line 140 mean?

16. Note in the next five lines how Arthur seems to feel the emptiness of all his work, the unreality of himself and of everything. How does Bedivere try to cheer him?

17. In what sense does the King mean, " My house hath been my doom," line 154?

18. What is Arthur's last deed before he falls?

19. With line 170 begins the first-published part of the *Idylls*. Note the sonorous, rolling quality of the opening. What is the scene pictured here? What feelings does it stir in you?

20. What things does Arthur recall of the golden days in Camelot? What story of Excalibur did you read in the first Idyll? What command does the King give Bedivere?

21. Read aloud lines 213–219. Which seem best to you? Which, if any, suggest the idea by their sound? This whole

passage, like lines 170–180, and many others in this Idyll, is what is called *romantic;* do you know what that means? If not, consult a dictionary, your teacher, or any other authorities you can.

22. In lines 220–233, which lines excel in giving a picture? Which in the effect of sound?

23. How does the King know that Bedivere deceived him? How does he rebuke him? How does Bedivere the second time justify to himself his disobedience?

24. Note lines 273–4. Tennyson himself thought these lines were very good. Can you see why? Would you have selected them as fine poetry?

25. Explain the meaning of lines 275–277; of line 278.

26. How does Arthur's second rebuke differ from his first? Explain line 289. How does Bedivere this time make sure of obedience? What happens when he flings the sword? What lines in the description would you select as finest? Read aloud lines 301–315. What lines seem, in their movement, swift or slow, to suit the action?

27. Read aloud lines 344–360. Point out in them some of the qualities you have already had called to your attention in other lines; the romantic quality of the scene, the way the lines express the idea not only by what they say but by their sound and movement, and especially the fine transition or change in the last seven. Select the lines that you think most impressive.

28. Read aloud lines 361–371. Comment upon them as upon the preceding passage. What are some of the most suggestive words in these lines?

29. What or who do you suppose the three queens were? See the *Introduction*, page 12.

30. Lines 408–410 are among the best known in all Tennyson's poetry. What do they mean? How do they apply to Arthur's work, and to the work of other leaders that came after? Can you think of some order or system that is now changing, "yielding place to new"? Or of some

"good custom" no longer good for the world? Commit these lines to memory.

31. Commit to memory also lines 418–423. What do they mean?

32. What was Avilion? Compare it with the Islands of the Blest, or the Garden of the Hesperides, in Greek mythology.

33. Read the last two paragraphs aloud. What do the last two lines suggest? Compare lines 408–410.

34. Review in your mind the four Idylls in this volume: What were Arthur's hopes and plans in the beginning? What work did he set himself to do? What interfered with his success and finally destroyed his kingdom? Which of his friends were false, which true? Does the conflict of right and wrong, this account of "Sense at war with Soul," as Tennyson phrased it, which runs through the whole story, end in victory for the evil, or is it implied that good will triumph in the end?

35. Or, does the chivalric and romantic part of the story interest you more than the moral of the stories? If so, what characters, what actions, what scenes can you recall? What pictures have you hung up in the gallery of your memory? Can you call before your mind, for instance, the mythical coming of Arthur on a wave of the sea and his mythical departure in the boat with the three black-robed queens? Or the picture of Gareth approaching Camelot? Or Elaine's body steered up the river into the city? Or the marriage of Arthur, with the mailed warriors around him shouting their battle-song? Or the ruined shrine, the place of tombs, the dim and misty night of midwinter when Arthur lay dying? What other pictures can you recall?

36. Or, if you take pleasure in things well said, what lines have stuck in your memory? What phrases give you pleasure by coming back to you? What things would you like to have been able to say as well?

Readers of the *Idylls* should know also these poems of Tennyson's: —

SIR GALAHAD

My good blade carves the casques
    of men,
My tough lance thrusteth sure,
My strength is as the strength of
    ten,
    Because my heart is pure.
The shattering trumpet shrilleth
    high,
    The hard brands shiver on the
      steel,
The splinter'd spear-shafts crack
    and fly,
    The horse and rider reel;
They reel, they roll in clanging
    lists,
    And when the tide of combat
      stands,
Perfume and flowers fall in
    showers,
    That lightly rain from ladies'
      hands.

How sweet are looks that ladies
    bend
    On whom their favors fall!
For them I battle till the end,
    To save from shame and thrall;
But all my heart is drawn
    above,
    My knees are bow'd in crypt
      and shrine;
I never felt the kiss of love,
    Nor maiden's hand in mine.
More bounteous aspects on me
    beam,
    Me mightier transports move
      and thrill;
So keep I fair thro' faith and
    prayer
    A virgin heart in work and
      will.

When down the stormy crescent
    goes,
    A light before me swims,
Between dark stems the forest
    glows,
    I hear a noise of hymns.
Then by some secret shrine I ride;
    I hear a voice, but none are
      there;
The stalls are void, the doors are
    wide,
    The tapers burning fair.
Fair gleams the snowy altar-cloth,
    The silver vessels sparkle clean,
The shrill bell rings, the censer
    swings,
    And solemn chants resound be-
      tween.

Sometimes on lonely mountain-
    meres
    I find a magic bark;
I leap on board; no helmsman
    steers;
    I float till all is dark.
A gentle sound, an awful light!
    Three angels bear the Holy
      Grail:
With folded feet, in stoles of
    white,
    On sleeping wings they sail.
Ah, blessed vision! blood of God!
    My spirit beats her mortal bars,
As down dark tides the glory
    slides,
    And star-like mingles with the
      stars.

When on my goodly charger borne
    Thro' dreaming towns I go,
The cock crows ere the Christmas
    morn,
    The streets are dumb with snow.

The tempest crackles on the
     leads,
   And, ringing, springs from brand
     and mail;
But o'er the dark a glory spreads,
   And gilds the driving hail.
I leave the plain, I climb the
     height;
   No branchy thicket shelter
     yields;
But blessed forms in whistling
     storms
   Fly o'er waste fens and windy
     fields.

A maiden knight — to me is given
   Such hope, I know not fear;
I yearn to breathe the airs of
     heaven
   That often meet me here.
I muse on joy that will not cease,
   Pure spaces clothed in living
     beams,
Pure lilies of eternal peace,
   Whose odors haunt my dreams;
And, stricken by an angel's hand,
   This mortal armor that I wear,
This weight and size, this heart
     and eyes,
   Are touch'd, are turn'd to finest
     air.

The clouds are broken in the sky,
   And thro' the mountain-walls
A rolling organ-harmony
   Swells up, and shakes and falls.
Then move the trees, the copses
     nod,
   Wings flutter, voices hover
     clear:
"O just and faithful knight of
     God!
   Ride on! the prize is near."
So pass I hostel, hall, and grange;
   By bridge and ford, by park and
     pale,

All-arm'd I ride, whate'er betide,
   Until I find the Holy Grail.

SIR LAUNCELOT AND
QUEEN GUINEVERE

A FRAGMENT

LIKE souls that balance joy and
     pain,
With tears and smiles from heaven
     again
The maiden Spring upon the plain
Came in a sunlit fall of rain.
   In crystal vapor everywhere
Blue isles of heaven laugh'd be-
     tween,
And far, in forest-deeps unseen,
The topmost elm-tree gather'd
     green
   From draughts of balmy air.

Sometimes the linnet piped his
     song:
Sometimes the throstle whistled
     strong:
Sometimes the sparhawk, wheel'd
     along,
Hush'd all the groves from fear of
     wrong:
   By grassy capes with fuller
     sound
In curves the yellowing river ran,
And drooping chestnut-buds be-
     gan
To spread into the perfect fan,
   Above the teeming ground.

Then, in the boyhood of the year,
Sir Launcelot and Queen Guine-
     vere
Rode thro' the coverts of the
     deer,
With blissful treble ringing clear.
   She seem'd a part of joyous
     Spring:

A gown of grass-green silk she
    wore,
Buckled with golden clasps be-
    fore ;
A light-green tuft of plumes she
    bore
    Closed in a golden ring.

Now on some twisted ivy-net,
Now by some tinkling rivulet,
In mosses mixt with violet
Her cream-white mule his pastern
    set ;
    And fleeter now she skimm'd
      the plains
Than she whose elfin prancer
    springs
By night to eery warblings,
When all the glimmering moor
    land rings
    With jingling bridle-reins.

As she fled fast thro' sun and
    shade,
The happy winds upon her play'd,
Blowing the ringlet from the
    braid.
She look'd so lovely, as she sway'd
    The rein with dainty finger-
      tips,
A man had given all other bliss,
And all his worldly worth for this,
To waste his whole heart in one kiss
    Upon her perfect lips.

THE LADY OF SHALOTT

PART I

On either side the river lie
Long fields of barley and of rye,
That clothe the wold and meet the
    sky ;
And thro' the field the road runs
    by
    To many-tower'd Camelot ;

And up and down the people go,
Gazing where the lilies blow
Round an island there below,
    The island of Shalott.

Willows whiten, aspens quiver,
Little breezes dusk and shiver
Thro' the wave that runs forever
By the island in the river
    Flowing down to Camelot.
Four gray walls, and four gray
    towers,
Overlook a space of flowers,
And the silent isle imbowers
    The Lady of Shalott.

By the margin, willow-veil'd,
Slide the heavy barges trail'd
By slow horses ; and unhail'd
The shallop flitteth silken-sail'd
    Skimming down to Camelot ·
But who hath seen her wave her
    hand ?
Or at the casement seen her stand ?
Or is she known in all the land,
    The Lady of Shalott ?

Only reapers, reaping early
In among the bearded barley,
Hear a song that echoes cheerly,
From the river winding clearly ;
    Down to tower'd Camelot ;
And by the moon the reaper
    weary,
Piling sheaves in uplands airy,
Listening, whispers " 'Tis the fairy
    Lady of Shalott."

PART II

There she weaves by night and
    day
A magic web with colors gay.
She has heard a whisper say,
A curse is on her if she stay
    To look down to Camelot.

She knows not what the curse may
    be,
And so she weaveth steadily,
And little other care hath she,
    The Lady of Shalott.

And moving thro' a mirror clear
That hangs before her all the year,
Shadows of the world appear.
There she sees the highway near
    Winding down to Camelot;
There the river eddy whirls,
And there the surly village-churls,
And the red cloaks of market girls,
    Pass onward from Shalott.

Sometimes a troop of damsels glad,
An abbot on an ambling pad,
Sometimes a curly shepherd-lad,
Or long-hair'd page in crimson clad,
    Goes by to tower'd Camelot;
And sometimes thro' the mirror
    blue
The knights come riding two and
    two:
She hath no loyal knight and
    true,
    The Lady of Shalott.

But in her web she still delights
To weave the mirror's magic
    sights,
For often thro' the silent nights
A funeral, with plumes and lights
    And music, went to Camelot;
Or when the moon was overhead,
Came two young lovers lately
    wed;
"I am half sick of shadows," said
    The Lady of Shalott.

PART III

A BOW-SHOT from her bower-
    eaves,
He rode between the barley-
    sheaves,

The sun came dazzling thro' the
    leaves
And flamed upon the brazen
    greaves
Of bold Sir Lancelot.
A red-cross knight forever kneel'd
To a lady in his shield,
That sparkled on the yellow field,
    Beside remote Shalott.

The gemmy bridle glitter'd free,
Like to some branch of stars we see
Hung in the golden Galaxy.
The bridle bells rang merrily
    As he rode down to Camelot;
And from his blazon'd baldric
    slung
A mighty silver bugle hung,
And as he rode his armor rung,
    Beside remote Shalott.

All in the blue unclouded weather
Thick-jewell'd shone the saddle-
    leather,
The helmet and the helmet-feather
Burn'd like one burning flame to-
    gether,
    As he rode down to Camelot;
As often thro' the purple night,
Below the starry clusters bright,
Some bearded meteor, trailing
    light,
    Moves over still Shalott.

His broad clear brow in sunlight
    glow'd;
On burnish'd hooves his war-
    horse trode;
From underneath his helmet
    flow'd
His coal-black curls as on he rode,
    As he rode down to Camelot.
From the bank and from the river
He flash'd into the crystal mirror,
"Tirra lirra," by the river
    Sang Sir Lancelot.

She left the web, she left the
loom,
She made three paces thro' the
room,
She saw the water-lily bloom,
She saw the helmet and the
plume,
    She look'd down to Camelot.
Out flew the web and floated
wide ;
The mirror crack'd from side to
side ;
"The curse is come upon me,"
cried
    The Lady of Shalott.

PART IV

In the stormy east-wind straining,
The pale yellow woods were wan-
ing,
The broad stream in his banks
complaining,
Heavily the low sky raining
    Over tower'd Camelot;
Down she came and found a boat
Beneath a willow left afloat,
And round about the prow she
wrote
    The Lady of Shalott.

And down the river's dim expanse
Like some bold seër in a trance,
Seeing all his own mischance —
With a glassy countenance
    Did she look to Camelot.
And at the closing of the day
She loosed the chain, and down she
lay ;
The broad stream bore her far
away,
    The Lady of Shalott.

Lying, robed in snowy white,
That loosely flew to left and
right —

The leaves upon her falling
light —
Thro' the noises of the night
    She floated down to Camelot ;
And as the boat-head wound
along
The willowy hills and fields among,
They heard her singing her last
song,
    The Lady of Shalott.

Heard a carol, mournful, holy,
Chanted loudly, chanted lowly,
Till her blood was frozen slowly,
And her eyes were darken'd
wholly,
    Turn'd to tower'd Camelot.
For ere she reach'd upon the tide
The first house by the water-
side,
Singing in her song she died,
    The Lady of Shalott.

Under tower and balcony,
By garden-wall and gallery,
A gleaming shape she floated by,
Dead-pale between the houses
high,
    Silent into Camelot.
Out upon the wharfs they came,
Knight and burgher, lord and
dame,
And round the prow they read her
name,
    The Lady of Shalott.

Who is this ? and what is here ?
And in the lighted palace near
Died the sound of royal cheer ;
And they cross'd themselves for
fear,
    All the knights at Camelot:
But Lancelot mused a little space;
He said, "She has a lovely face :
God in his mercy lend her grace,
    The Lady of Shalott."

TEXTBOOKS IN CITIZENSHIP

GOVERNMENT AND POLITICS IN THE UNITED STATES. Problems of American Democracy. *A Textbook for Secondary Schools.*

By WILLIAM B. GUITTEAU, Ph.D., formerly Superintendent of Schools, Toledo, Ohio. With Illus. and Diagrams. Crown 8vo.

This book fully covers the requirements of modern high schools in regard to the teaching of Civics. It gives an adequate knowledge of the various forms of government, local, state, and national, emphasizing, however, the practical activities in which students are most interested, and the problems with which as citizens they will be most concerned. Questions at the end of each chapter give local applications of principles discussed in the text.

PREPARING FOR CITIZENSHIP. *An Elementary Textbook in Civics.*

By WILLIAM BACKUS GUITTEAU, Ph.D.

This is an admirable textbook for the upper grammar grades, and for the first year of the high school. It gives in simple language a very clear explanation of how and why governments are formed, what government does for the citizen, and what the citizen owes to his government. All necessary facts regarding local, state, and national government are given, with the main emphasis upon the practical aspects of government. The book concludes with an inspiring expression of our national ideals of self-reliance, equality of opportunity, education for all, and the promotion of international peace. Each chapter is accompanied by questions and exercises which will stimulate investigation on the part of pupils into the organization and functions of local government.

AMERICANIZATION AND CITIZENSHIP.

By HANSON HART WEBSTER.

Important and distinctive features of this book are: — (1) the catechism upon the United States Constitution; (2) the statement of the principles underlying our government; (3) the explanation of the duties and privileges of citizens. It is recommended as a valuable handbook for all Americans, both native and foreign-born.

HOUGHTON MIFFLIN COMPANY

PRACTICAL NEW TEXTBOOKS

PRACTICAL BUSINESS ENGLISH.

By Oscar C. Gallagher, Superintendent of Schools, Brookline, Mass., formerly Head Master, West Roxbury High School, Boston, and Leonard B. Moulton, Department of English, High School of Commerce, Boston.

Practical Business English tells how and what to write to conduct and promote business. Principles are presented clearly and definitely. Every exercise is so planned and analyzed that the pupil has a certain piece of work before him, with specific directions as to how to do it. Much of the material in the book is new and has no been treated in other books of similar character.

LA CLASSE EN FRANÇAIS.

By E. Gourio, Professor agrégé de l'Université de Paris, Chevalier de la Légion d'Honneur.

This book teaches pupils to read, speak, write, and think in French in a remarkably short time. It follows the direct method; that is, the entire book is written in French excepting translations of words and phrases, and the vocabulary at the end of the book. *La Classe en Français* provides numerous examples, definitions, and pictures to explain the meaning of new words.

A Manual for Teachers — "The Direct Method of Teaching French" — has been prepared to accompany *La Classe en Français*.

SPANISH TAUGHT IN SPANISH.

By Charles F. McHale, Instructor in Spanish in the National City Bank, New York.

The strong appeal of *Spanish Taught in Spanish* is that the pupil learns his lessons in Spanish right from the start. This method stimulates interest and thus enables the pupil to think in Spanish and to absorb the language with amazing rapidity.

THE SCIENCE OF EVERYDAY LIFE.

By Edgar F. Van Buskirk, formerly in charge of General Science, DeWitt Clinton High School, New York City, and Edith L. Smith, formerly Instructor, Geography Department, Boston Normal School.

This is the first science book to be built on a definite unifying principle. This basis is *Everyday Needs*. All the material is grouped under five units, which are subdivided into projects.

(1) *The Air and How We Use It.* — (2) *Water and How We Use It.* — (3) *Foods and How We Use Them.* — (4) *Protection — Homes and Clothing.* — (5) *The Work of the World.*

The course bears a close relation to the familiar conditions of the pupil's life. The applicability of what he is studying is constantly impressed upon his mind.

HOUGHTON MIFFLIN COMPANY

1954

64   554   319